Money: An Owner's Manual

A Personal Guide to Financial Freedom

By Dennis R. Deaton

MMI Publishing

Mesa, AZ

Money: An Owner's Manual
A Personal Guide to Financial Freedom
By Dennis R. Deaton

Editor: Cecily Markland

Assistant Editor: Susan S. Deaton

Cover Design: Georgie Stevens

Typesetting: Cecily Markland

Printed in the United States of America

First Printing, 1992

Second Printing, 1993

Orders and editorial correspondence should also be addressed to TimeMax, Inc.

Library of Congress Catalog Card Number 92-64320

ISBN 1-881840-25-5

TimeMax, Inc.
1818 E. Southern Avenue
Mesa, Arizona 85204
(602) 545-8311

Acknowledgments

The great force required in breaking new personal ground is seldom equalled on subsequent passages. Rarely is such energy generated solely by the individual. The achievement is accomplished through the melding of the will and effort of many. In the birthing of this book, there have been many who have labored.

I express my deepest appreciation to:

Reece A. Bawden, my unwavering and loyal partner, and **Clyde L. Bawden**, my talented colleague, both of whom diligently wrought while I wrote;

Cecily Markland for her careful editing, layout and design work, encouragement and counsel,

And,

Susan, my wife, whose faith, sacrifice and love has sustained me, replenished me and inspired me on every level.

With special appreciation to:

Ronald E. Tew who applied the final force to bring the book to publication through his conviction, means and unwillingness to let adversity prevail.

TABLE OF CONTENTS

FOREWORD

Anyone can be rich. I believe any reasonably intelligent, moderately educated person can walk the path to wealth and financial freedom. I become more convinced of that every day.

In preparing to write this book, I met and interviewed dozens of wealthy people. Each time, I came away with a renewed awareness: There is nothing innately exceptional or unusual about them. They are, virtually without exception, solid, genuine, salt-of-the-earth people with no distinguishing trademark. Yet they are "filthy rich," and they are free.

External characteristics have little bearing. It is not who they are, how they look, or where they work that sets the wealthy apart. It is how they think. It is their internal characteristics which make all the difference. They know exactly where they are going, and they apply fundamental principles to get there. The process is not complicated or mystical. In fact, it is amazingly simple.

Riches and wealth are effects. They do not occur spontaneously or randomly. They happen because they are caused to happen. Wealth is the due consequence of applied principles. While anyone can, and everyone should, be free of the shackles of Mammon, no one *will* shed those chains without conforming to these fundamental principles.

The difficulty of all of this is vastly overrated. There are means, described in this book, which can be employed to achieve the consistency and constancy which will yield financial freedom. Far from painful, they are exciting and invigorating. Best of all, they are so simple and easy to understand, anyone can do it— anyone, who really wants to, can achieve ample prosperity and financial peace of mind.

One of the most insidious and pervasive transgressions of this generation is to flaunt a lifestyle beyond one's actual means. With ample credit so readily available, many have unintentionally stumbled into a minefield of financial misery, trying to *seem*, rather than be, rich. In doing so, they have unwittingly set the stage for several long acts of human tragedy.

This book teaches how to have money—lots of it—piles of it. Yet it also intends to convince you that money and financial freedom are not perfectly synonymous. You can earn lots of money and never experience what it's like to be free. The world is obese with examples of that. I want to teach you to be financially free, not just appear to be.

When I wax philosophical about life, I can conceive of individuals who can be free and happy with very little money. But that is not my message either—to be purely philosophical about money. This book propounds the way to the genuine and palpable freedom that comes from having an abundant supply of cash while maintaining a healthy perspective about life and the actual sources of satisfaction and joy.

But, until the destination becomes vividly clear, there is no direct route. To have a complete understanding of "where" we are headed, we will certainly have to come to a mutual understanding of terms. Helping you crystallize valid definitions in your mind is partly what this book is about.

Assuredly, this book is also about "how." How to do it. How to do it in a simple, direct, fail-safe way. You are going to be given every technique and tool you need to accumulate money and achieve financial freedom.

However, this book goes well beyond that. Socrates said, "Teach me sufficiently why a thing should be done, and I will move heaven and earth to do it." So, this book has a lot to say about "what" and "why" as well. Without a vividly clear perspective of "what" and "why," people are not able to stay with the "how" long enough to reap the harvest.

Vision begets action, and correct vision begets not just action but victory. Once you see plainly what must be done and why it will work, over half the battle has been won. This book helps you do that—to see it and to live it. It debunks myths, disrobes scams and traps, clarifies issues and enunciates perspectives. It delineates correct principles, and tutors simple, straightforward methods of applying them. Most importantly, it explains how to make it all work in daily life.

Full financial freedom is worth the effort. It is a reward worth wanting and working for—worth seeking. You will discover that once you know what to seek, where to seek and how, you will find.

SECTION I

THE PITFALLS

You can not find until you know what you seek.

The principal reason most people do not achieve genuine financial freedom is that they do not define what they are really after. They fail, primarily and precisely, because they have never clarified in their minds where they are going and, more importantly, why. As a consequence they become lost in a maze of circuitous routes and blind alleys. Section I will help you to establish correct monetary objectives and alert you to some of the most abrupt dead ends in the modern monetary labyrinth.

CHAPTER 1

Down to Money

Bill should have been governor. He would have been great. It would have been good for him, good for the state and good for the people living there. He is honest and competent and indefatigable. It was his dream, but he did not even run for office.

Karen has regrets, too. She wishes she had gone to medical school. She would have been a great doctor. She is empathetic, wise and extremely intelligent. Thousands of people could have benefited and lived better lives through her ministrations. It was her dream, but she did not even apply for medical school.

The same thing thwarted Karen that thwarted Bill: perceptions about money. Neither thought they had the financial resources to pursue their dreams. It all came down to money.

On the other hand, Tom *did* go to medical school and is a doctor in a bustling clinic. But he is not very happy. He only tolerates the practice of medicine. Tom became a doctor because he thought it was a good, secure way to make big money. When he was growing up, all of the doctors in his home town lived in large, beautiful homes in the poshest neighborhoods. They drove the most expensive cars and wore the finest clothes. What is more, these doctors were never unemployed. People got sick and injured in good economic times and in bad. A doctor's income appeared to be recession-proof. So Tom made his decision. Once again it came down to money.

Mark and Sally are disappointed with their daughter's fiance'. He is personable and bright, but he is not well-to-do. He lives in an apartment and is toiling to get through college. His parents, too, live in modest circumstances. They own a small home in a tract subdivision and have made no secret of the fact that they have struggled all their lives. Mark and Sally are just not sure the young man is good enough for their daughter. They may not even realize it consciously, but the source of their apprehension stems from their perspectives about money.

Not long ago, my six-year-old son spoke excitedly at the dinner table. He had met the new boy in the neighborhood. "He's a really neat guy, Dad. He has a Nintendo with all the games, and wears Air Jordan sneakers, and has a $300 racing bike." It has not taken him long in life to pick up on the cues. Even a six-year-old has figured it out: "Neat" is inseparably connected to "has" and "wears."

It always seems to come down to money.

It seems that almost everyone these days is driving down the highway of life with impaired faculties. We are out of control, having imbibed the intoxicating wine labeled, "MONEY knows best."

MONEY has become the sole manager and magistrate. MONEY permits or MONEY denies. Mom says to Dad, "I think Daughter has a gift for music. She wants to take piano lessons. What do you think?" Dad's first question: "How much will it cost?" The answer, high or low, determines Dad's posture. (Sure, Dad's in favor of Daughter getting whatever she needs and deserves, but it's MONEY that decides.)

Dad says to Mom, "Son has his heart set on college. He wants to go to Yale." Mom responds, "That's impossible! Yale is too expensive. You will have to talk some sense into him. He is not being realistic." The implication is clear: MONEY decrees reality. MONEY utters the final word—nothing can overrule MONEY. MONEY *always* knows best.

MONEY has become the ultimate judge in our society. What MONEY says, goes. It decides what is possible and what is infeasible. Cold cash alone is allowed to define "reality"—to determine what is realistic and what is idle dreaming. The size of our purse determines where we go, when we depart, how fast we get there, how long we stay. MONEY enacts or vetoes every plan, holds final say on every act. It has become the compass by which people take their bearings and the yardstick by which they make their measurements.

MONEY has somehow weaseled its way to supremacy. It does not deserve all this respect. Yet, it influences how people see the world, how they view and esteem their fellows; it even shapes what they think of themselves. MONEY has become the exclusive meter of value and success. In too many eyes, self-worth is synonymous with net worth.

But it's not MONEY's fault.

How did MONEY get so much authority? How can it wield such power? In actuality, MONEY is as inanimate as a brick. Although we seem to be doing our utmost to give money a persona, it does not have one. It is not *MONEY* after all; it is simply, money.

MONEY THOUGHTS

So what is money? Is money a faithful friend or an enemy? Is it a servant or a slave driver? A blight on mankind's soul or a blessing from heaven? Ask anyone, "Will money solve problems?" "Oh, yes!" they will say, "If I had money, I could leave all my problems behind. I could go and do everything I really want to do."

Ask again, "Does money cause misery and problems?" "Yes," they will respond, "Wouldn't the world be great if we weren't haggling over money all the time?" Poor money. It doesn't know what we think. We say it frees us. We say it enslaves us. We love it. We hate it. That money doesn't have a complex over all this is a wonder.

The reason money does not have a complex is obvious. It does not think. A dollar bill does not know how I feel about it, or how you do. It does not care if I own it, if you own it, or if anyone else owns it. It does not care if it's saved or spent, or what it is spent on. Totally indifferent to our love or lust, money does not care whether it comes or goes or stays. Very dispassionate is money.

Ultimately, we must come to admit that money has no behavior outside our own. Money does not think. *We* think. (That is, we are supposed to.) When we think, it is what we choose to think about that matters. Thought precedes action in every aspect of human behavior. Everything we do, we do first in our minds. Our thoughts are the seeds of our actions. They make us or break us. How clearly we think those thoughts also matters. The clearer the vision, the more predictable and dependable the outcome.

The mind can envision and achieve superlative things when rightly directed. I have learned (and it is emphatically re-substantiated every day) that the trademark of high achievers is FOCUS. They exert laser-like concentration on their chosen objectives. They are not gifted with more brains; they simply utilize them more selectively. They eliminate the distractions and vanquish the preoccupations which divert and deflect others from optimum performance.

Clear thinking is what this book is about—clear thinking about money. When people get their bearings straight and think clearly about money, they become money wise. Being money wise, they avoid innumerable problems and wind up owning money—lots of it, instead of money owning them. More importantly, they attain wisdom about other things. They become wise enough to think about things other than money—things which matter a great deal more than money. In the end, they become very wise and "filthy rich" in ways that far transcend money.

Nothing preoccupies the mind like worry over money. It is the number one thief of creative genius. Most people are so distracted thinking and worrying about money and related material concerns, they fail to think about anything else. The tragedy lies in what we could be doing with that same mental focus and energy.

GRIM STATISTICS

Money distractions are at the root of much that ails us. The American Bar Association estimates over 85 percent of all divorces are money-management related. Pat B. Brian, a prominent attorney, believes that statistic is too low. He says:

> When one gets to the unraveling of the "Gordian Knot" of marital conflict, it is found that the number one killer of marital happiness is money related. In divorce after divorce, the underlying cause is undisciplined money management.

Nothing siphons our energy "on the job" like financial distress "in the home." The wasted, squandered productivity in this country alone is quantitatively incalculable. Even rough estimates suggest staggering annual losses.

The 1989 U.S. Department of Commerce Income and Poverty Report conveyed statistics which should sober all of us. For every 100 U.S. citizens born in 1923 the following actual profile existed when the age group reached retirement (age 65): Twenty-nine were deceased. Fourteen had annual incomes *under* $5,000! (That is below the poverty level.) Fifty-one had incomes ranging from $5,000 to $25,000. That sounds a little better until you realize the income for the large majority in this range was under $15,000 per year. (That is not exactly soaring over the poverty level.) Only five in a hundred enjoyed a modestly comfortable income of $25,000 to $50,000 annually, and only one— one in a hundred—had an annual income in excess of $50,000.

The litany is virtually endless. The U.S. Social Security Administration states that almost 90 percent of the people in this country enter retirement with less than $500 in their bankbooks. One authority reports a truly mind-shocking statistic that there are more men worth $100 at age 18 than there are at age 65—meaning, in effect, that most people do not even save $2 a year during nearly 50 years of economic productivity!

Most of the retired men and women in this country of wealth are not really enjoying "golden" years. After working all their lives for the carefree days of retirement, they actually find themselves more financially strapped than ever. Instead of traveling at will, spending time with family and friends, splurging on a gift or two for their grandchildren, they find themselves living on a less-than-modest, fixed income. For many, it is a burden too painful to admit. They suffer in silence.

All of that collides with the fact that we live in the wealthiest country in all the world with opportunity abounding. The ironic truth is most Americans will have many hundreds of thousands, if not several millions, of dollars run through their hands during their productive years. Why do they wind up poor?

THE CRUX

People say they are willing to do anything to have money. And, some of them prove it. Some people will cheat, lie, steal and embezzle. They will perjure themselves; defraud friends, partners or employers; marry for money; divorce for money; and betray their country for money. They will counterfeit, extort, kidnap and commit murder—literally go to hell and throw away the key—for money. What most people will not do—what they flatly refuse to do—is muster a little self-discipline.

The wisdom of the ages still applies: Those who fail to master themselves fall prey to all others. In terms of money this is especially true. If you don't own your money, money will own you. Ralph Waldo Emerson said, "Money can be an obedient servant, but a harsh taskmaster." You can master money or be slave to it. You have the option, but it is one or the other.

The crux of all this lies in the simple fact that money is not animate and has no behavior of its own. Money has no demeanor outside your own conduct. What money does or does not do is entirely dependent on you.

To put it plainly: Money mastery is self-mastery. You have got to learn to control you. You are the one with the mind and the will to act or not act. Money does not come and go by itself. You bring it in and either keep it or disburse it. Since you are the one with the mind, unless, and until, you are willing to manage yourself, you are going to experience multitudes of self-inflicted wounds. When it comes to money, there is no substitute for self-discipline. And, self-discipline is none other than mind management.

MAPS IN THE MIND

The key to effective mind management is vision—clear vision. I am absolutely convinced that the major reason most people labor (and labor) in vain for financial freedom is they lack a crystal-clear vision of what they are after.

Consider the following two truths about the mind:

(1) The mind does not solve GENERAL problems.

(2) The mind does not achieve VAGUE OR GENERAL goals.

When presented with generalities, the creative mechanism stalls. The mind pauses, pending clarifying details.

On the other hand, give the mind *a specific* set of parameters, a *specific* problem, a *specific* objective or goal, and stand back. The mind will go to work and achieve amazing, stunning breakthroughs. The ingenuity and innovative-creative capabilities of our minds are not just remarkable, they are downright miraculous. When objectives are vivid and clear, ideas are generated, methods are defined, energy is released, action ensues, and achievement results.

Most people fail to achieve financial freedom primarily, and precisely, because they hold only vague or general images of what they are really trying to accomplish. They know it has something to do with money—lots of it—and they go charging after it. They earn. They connive. They gamble and (pardon the redundancy here) they invest. Yet withal, their target is ill-defined and their objective is broad and vague. They never define "how much," "what for," or "why." Thus, they never arrive. They only pursue.

If the destination is only defined as "more money," the map will be filled with confusing intersections and by-ways. Circuitous routes leading to dead ends and frustration will be inevitable. The journey will be anything but direct and efficient. Last, and most importantly, the journey to "more money" is an endless odyssey. It never ends because there is no specific destination. Contrary to the commonly exhibited behavior, life is not supposed to be a never-ending pursuit of cash until death puts an abrupt termination to it. You will not know financial freedom until, somehow and sometime, you no longer pursue it.

You may be asking yourself introspective questions right now about where your own mind is set. Here's a little self-discovery test which may help. Picture the following scenario: Suppose today you were to receive in the mail an unexpected surprise—a check for $25,000, tax free. On a sheet of paper, write down exactly what you would do with the money. You have the freedom to do whatever you wish. You can break it down into smaller sums, parcel or subdivide it any way you choose. What would you do with $25,000 today? Don't be noble; be honest. And, don't ponder it. It is your first impulse which is so instructive. What would your real tendencies be? Where would you allot the cash?

There are no firm absolutes. Individual circumstances can make an immense difference, and, in this situation, to teach a principle, I will generalize. All that understood, if you said, "Put it into savings," I commend you. That is a good sign. To me, that is an indication that you are resisting a widespread trap of our generation: "Work to earn, and earn to spend."

If your first inclination was to apply the $25,000 to your debts, I commend you, too. If you are going to have monetary peace of mind—if you are ever going to know what it's like to be free of all the preoccupation over money—you have got to vanquish debt and deficit spending. That is not an option.

If you said, "I'm really not sure," and nothing came immediately to mind, your objectives are not defined. You may not be a spend-thrift, but neither are you focused.

Finally, if you were tempted to expend, to make some long-yearned-for purchase or acquisition, even in the name of "investment," your mind set needs adjustment. If your first impulse was not to hang on to the money, your objectives plead for serious re-evaluation.

My purpose here is not to moralize but to sharpen your focus *on* your focus. Again, I am absolutely convinced the chief reason most people never arrive is they do not have a precise vision of the destination in the first place.

DIRECTIONS TO UTOPIA

Suppose we take, for example, a couple living in California who decide to journey to a distant city, Utopia, Nova Scotia. They are not precisely sure of the most direct route, but they have the impression that the faster they get started, the better. (They want to arrive while they still have time to enjoy it, you know. "Life is short—doesn't go on forever.") So with a barely subdued sense of urgency, they depart, thinking that along the way they will surely be able to acquire the necessary instructions to arrive directly and in good time.

As they journey, they are delighted to discover that just about everyone they meet has helpful suggestions on how to get to Utopia, Nova Scotia. It is utterly remarkable how many people seem to know the *exact* route. Most people are actually quite fervent about it. Although many of them, when totally candid on the subject, admit they haven't actually been there themselves, they, nonetheless, provide ample assurances that they *know* the way.

They state that they have learned from the very best authorities and most reliable sources the precise route. Many report having actually traveled a good share of the way to Utopia by way of an ingenious shortcut. They take particular pride in explaining that this shortcut is novel and exclusive and that very few other maps include this advantageous new route.

Undaunted by the fact that much of the data contradicts itself, our upright pair listen, ponder, and assemble what they think is an ideal map. Most of the highways on the map are highly recommended by authoritative people whose credentials almost speak for themselves. The highways they recommend, in fact, are teeming with travelers which seems to validate their claims. The truth is, sadly, major parts of the map are wrong. Some parts are actually concocted to benefit the "map makers." (You could call these "toll roads.")

Map in hand, our enthusiastic couple pursues their journey. They are positive, energetic people and are sure if anyone can make it to Utopia in good time, it is surely they. Despite their sincerity and impeccable intentions, the map is still erroneous. It is an inaccurate map. It is vague in places and downright mistaken in others. What happens to our diligent pair if they follow this inaccurate map? They get lost.

BUT, let's suppose they get up a half-hour earlier every morning, increase the intensity and fervor of their efforts, travel longer hours, cut down on their rest stops, push and press ahead, and earnestly adhere to the routes of their inaccurate map. Then what happens?

They get lost *faster*.

MORAL: WHEN IT COMES TO GETTING YOUR BEARINGS AND STAYING ON COURSE, THE MAP IS EVERYTHING.

CHAPTER 2

The Difference That Makes The Difference

Have you ever attended a Pro-Am golf tournament, where amateurs match their skills with the real professionals? It is one of my favorite things to do. You can learn a lot by attending such an event. Not just about golf either. You can learn a lot about life, and about success and failure. Most of the time I do not know any of the amateurs when I first arrive. But sooner or later I wind up rooting for one or two of them. A closet underdog myself, I love to see the "little guy" succeed. Even as a boy I could never get myself to cheer for the Celtics in basketball and, in baseball, I absolutely detested the Yankees. It is much more exciting to pull for the "Davids" than the "Goliaths," even though the Goliaths usually prevail.

Watching skilled amateurs compete against the best in the sport, something has become clear to me: In most respects, the pros are not dramatically superior to the obscure contenders. In fact, many amateurs have better technique and are stronger physically than their idols. Once in a while these young athletes win. Their stronger bodies and near-perfect swings *do* triumph but not very often. Over 95 percent of the time, the pros win.

If the amateurs are as good or better technically and are stronger physically, why do they not win more often?

They do not, because for success and victory, might and energy are not the only criteria. Not even technique is the pivotal factor. There is something that outranks those elements. The pros have this something while the amateurs are still in the process of acquiring it. This difference makes the difference.

Where the pros prevail—where they have dramatic superiority over the amateurs—is in *the mind*. The pros are superior mentally. They have better mental maps. They have a competent certainty about themselves which originates deep within. They have a sense of control. They generally do not become flustered or upset when they hit a poor shot or some other factor goes awry. They concentrate. They are not awed by the attention or distracted by the crowd. They are centered on what they are doing and how they are going to do it.

That is why they win and why they win consistently. They do not carry the map in their golf bag or have it written on the back of their caddie's shirt. It is indelibly imprinted in their minds. It is part of them—an integral part of their walk and talk. That is the crucial characteristic of real pros.

Without question, the same is true in the realm of money. Those who succeed in financial matters are following a superior mental map. Not written on their sleeve, they possess inwardly a precise vision of their financial objective and strategy. The definiteness of their vision is what sets them apart from those who do not succeed. Monetary "pros" have thought the course through many times in their mind. They know where the traps and water hazards lie, and they see clearly how they are going to play the course to avoid them. The financial amateurs lack the mental insight, the foresight, and they wind up just playing a stroke at a time. They do not have a comprehensive strategy for the whole course. The pros see a bigger picture and know how to avoid the penalties that thwart the lesser players.

When it comes to money, one of the grand insights to the course is very subtle in nature. The pros see this subtlety. The novices often fail to recognize the superiority of this mind set, even after it has been told to them. Sometimes it's the most basic of things that trips us up.

KEY WORDS—KEY CONCEPTS

The primordial concept in a correct mental map about money hinges on two key words. The first one is ACQUIRE-MENT. A dictionary supplies the definition:

> Acquirement - n. The act of obtaining. The gaining posses-
> sion of; getting by one's own efforts or exertion.

When it comes to money, an acquirement mind set is the norm. It is the most popular and most highly recommended strategy in the world today. Everywhere you turn someone is selling you a way to get your hands on more cash. That alone should speak volumes. Most people are totally focused on "getting or obtaining," and they err. Acquirement is the *wrong* destination. Those who possess the acquirement mind set wind up playing in the rough.

The rich people I have studied have rejected that map. They have thought things through, and they have looked far enough ahead to see where that road leads. The financially free, the ones I studied and interviewed, were not obsessively focused on the acquirement of more money. Theirs was a better way. In the final analysis, I am convinced that most of them succeeded precisely because they were *not* centered on acquirement.

I have come to resent the mentality that promotes and prescribes accelerated acquirement as the solution to monetary problems. Accelerated acquirement actually amplifies the stress. It exacts physical, mental, moral and spiritual tolls. That strategy hardly has to be recommended. The world is full of people obsessed with acquirement. They are feverishly ransacking the world, pushing relentlessly for *more*. "More what?" you may ask them. "Not sure. Doesn't matter. More!" they respond. They are unremittingly pursuing, driving themselves to early graves in the quest for more. *That* is definitely a false map.

Accelerated acquirement is not the medicine, because *insufficient acquirement is not the disease.* In the United States, most of us have no problem acquiring money. It rolls through our fingers at mind-boggling rates. There lies the crux, and the irony is poignant. Focusing on accelerated acquirement is actually the malady contributing to these ills. It is not acquiring the stuff (money) which is the issue, most of us simply can not manage to hang on to much of it. Which brings us to the second key word: ACCUMULATION.

> Accumulation - n. The act of amassing or gathering. To mount up, as into a great heap or pile.

Think of it. ACCUMULATION. Visualize yourself actually amassing a large amount of money—gathering, as into a great heap or pile, a large quantity of friendly greenbacks. Try it. Picture yourself amassing and possessing a nice, generous pile of crisp, clean money.

If you are following my suggestion literally, you are undoubtedly sporting a warm, comfortable smile right now. The image of stockpiling a Matterhorn of money is a fairly therapeutic thought in our stress-filled lives. And, that is my point: The vision of acquirement is stressful. The vision of accumulation is reassuring. This is the book on accumulation—how to amass and retain—stock up and stash away—enough cash so you can step down off the "acquirement treadmill," and live.

The distinction goes beyond semantics. Visualizing accumulation, not just acquirement, is more than an objective, it is the key. Understanding that simple mental distinction not only specifies the route, but it starts to clarify a measurable, attainable destination. We gain an important insight: Accumulation and acquirement are not adjacent lanes on the same highway. They are actually entirely different highways, heading in different directions. As Robert Frost aptly penned, "...two roads diverged in a wood...I took the one less traveled by, and that has made all the difference." People who can foresee the difference between the road to acquirement and the road to accumulation conquer half the frontier right there. Conversely, failure to maintain that perspective is fatal. You can acquire until you are old and gray but never know serenity.

A CASE IN POINT

I have a very good friend who learned the hard way where the road to acquirement goes. By profession, he is a physician with a high volume practice. When he opened his practice, it thrived rapidly. He had selected a growing community and, for a time, was the only practitioner in his specialty for miles. He was a good, conscientious doctor and enjoyed what everyone in the community thought was a skyrocketing medical practice.

We had a good friendship, but we didn't live in the same city, so weeks would go by without seeing each other. We tried to stay in touch by getting together a couple of times a year. On one such occasion, I began discussing a financial idea I was developing when he delivered a thunderbolt revelation. I had tapped a reservoir of pent-up emotions and he began to pour out an inventory of personal woes. He thought he could make it through a period of "tight cash flow" with a note to "catch up on some bills." But, his financial balance sheet was such a shambles, no bank in the state would go with him on a note. If he could not get help somewhere, he was facing bankruptcy.

He went on to describe severe marital problems which he thought would probably eventuate in divorce. The more he talked and disclosed his heavy financial burdens, the more he sounded like an exhausted, totally drained human being. His verve and enthusiasm for life were gone. Hardly a flicker of fight remained. Over and over, he'd mutter, "I've had it. It's been this way for months. I've tried to fight my way out of it. I've been going 90 miles an hour for so long, I just can't give it any more. I've had it."

He then proceeded to recount the history of a downward spiral to his present state of despair. He had accrued sizeable debts in getting through medical school which were followed by the costs and debts of setting up a practice with a new office building, furnishings and equipment.

As the practice took off, and with such great prospects ahead, he decided to plunge into the construction of a luxurious home. He and his wife had "struggled like paupers" to get through school, he reasoned, and it was time to get into the home they deserved—one that he felt would "fit the image" of a prospering physician.

Not long after, with the demand for his services increasing, and personal needs for cash mounting, it seemed apparent to him that expanding the practice was warranted. He needed a larger, nicer facility with more space (and, of course, more image). A choice lot was financed (do not read "purchased") at a healthy price. A new clinic was built, first through construction financing, then with a long-term loan. All this he was doing with the help and emphatic encouragement of his bankers, accountants and financial advisers. He had a great future, could write off the interest and "shelter" some income. It all seemed so good, on paper. But, in reality, it brought more debt which meant greater pressure on the cash flow of his practice to service that debt.

With the lion's share of his income going to debt service, he often felt a little cheated in his spendable dollars. Here he was, a busy physician, with precious few surplus dollars, having to worry about meeting monthly obligations. Even though his practice was strong and healthy he was "maxing out," and he could see that he was going to be strapped to these obligations a long way into the future.

Under that load, as weeks began to run into months, the harness began to chafe a bit and he found himself splurging on expensive toys from time to time. He needed them "to get away from the rat race," he rationalized. With few discretionary dollars available, the toys, too, were financed.

After a while, growing impatient with the slow growth of spendable money, he ventured into some speculative investments which he thought would get him "over the hump" and, at the same time, create even more tax shelter. The money for these "investments" was squeezed out of cash flow from his practice and he noticed his accounts payable gradually, steadily rising each month.

Unfortunately, these investments failed to perform as expected, and, rather than prospering, they added to the burden. Some of the "investments" began demanding money.

He consoled himself with the hope that the negative cash flow was only temporary and things would soon turn around and his investments would start adding to the solution rather than contributing to the problem. "Besides," he rationalized, "a lot of that money would just be going to taxes anyway," and his tax liability was modest compared to many of his colleagues.

Some of his ventures went completely belly up. He lost a chunk of money here and a chunk there. These losses were written off his taxes, and he dressed his wounds with "tax reduction salve." The losses and negative cash flow extracted by his investments markedly added to the pressure on the practice. Each month the practice had to produce more.

The next symptom that appeared was the saddest of all. He reported that he began to abhor his profession. The financial pressure dictated higher output, which, in turn, increased the tension and friction. Soon, "going to the office" was synonymous with leaping on the treadmill and "gutting out another day." As a result, the love for his work died. Naturally, the quality of his performance diminished. He wasn't the vibrant, personable doctor he once was. Although nothing was so distinct that the patients could put a finger on it, they sensed something was missing and some of them started looking elsewhere for services.

This reduced the income, which increased the pressure, which reduced his vitality, which decreased his performance, which affected the demand for his services, which reduced the income, which increased the pressure....He found himself in a tragic tailspin, spiraling downward, until one day there was a crash.

There he sat exhausted—burnt-out—totally spent mentally, physically, emotionally and financially. He had earned millions of dollars, but had accrued no savings—not a dime. His debts had grown annually. He was paying on a huge home, a couple of expensive automobiles, and some expensive toys; and he was miserable.

I made attempts at cheering him up. It was then that I learned that my optimistic friend of the past had vanished somewhere along the line and had been supplanted with a less amicable character. He was now a pessimistic, cynical wreck. He had reduced his life qualitatively and probably quantitatively as well.

One of his parting comments revealed a lot, "I wonder now why I even went into medicine at all. I thought it would provide a comfortable life for me and my family. If I had known this was what it would be like, I would have gone into ditch digging. To think I went through the long grind of medical school for this."

THERE IS TRAGEDY AHEAD FOR THOSE WHO FOLLOW INCORRECT MAPS. My friend had become a World Class Acquirer.

THE LAWS OF ACCUMULATION

One of the greatest ironies of life is that the most profound and powerful principles are astonishingly simple. In whatever endeavor, the person who consistently excels is the one who, in the final analysis, gets down to the basics and masters the fundamentals. In this over-communicated society, too often we lose sight of that fact. There is so much hyperbolic rhetoric filling the air, the fundamental truths of human happiness have become obscured, and confusion reigns. There exists as never before a crying need to reaffirm simple, correct principles in money management.

And now, prepare for the utmost in simple, comprehensible financial strategy. (I have tried in vain to make this part of the book complicated.) There are only two laws that have to be applied in order to accumulate money:

LAW NO. 1: DON'T SPEND ALL YOU EARN.

LAW NO. 2: DON'T LOSE WHAT YOU SAVE.

You do not have to be Marilyn vos Savant to understand these principles. You do not have to subscribe to savvy newsletters. You do not have to graduate cum laude from Harvard Business School, be a clairvoyant, or be excessively talented, beautiful or slim. All you have to do is follow that simple map.

CHAPTER 3

The Lure of Alternate Routes

The road to financial freedom is astoundingly simple. No duplicity or ambiguity here; disorientation should not occur. However, let us not be too naive. We don't want to confuse the map for the territory.

We are negotiating passage over tricky topography. When one looks up from the simple "Map of Accumulation," one immediately comes to realize that there are numerous confusing intersections. There are clever vendors at every turn, hawking other maps—more colorfully painted—heralding "easier" routes. Many map makers spare no expense on "PR work" to get us to take their well-traveled toll roads. Everywhere we turn there are enticing detours luring us from our discreet objectives. The territory is fraught with counterfeit thoroughfares and smooth voices courting accedence.

In addition, some map makers do not hesitate to openly condemn our simple little map. It not only lacks sophistication, they say, but overlooks some of the realities of the terrain. Yes, we can get to financial freedom by following that plan, they admit, but it will take too much time. Their way is so much quicker and easier. Temptation is strong to timorously fold our map and put it aside in favor of one of the more stylish plans on the midway.

Before we do so, however, let us review the thoroughfares most offered—the routes on the most commonly heralded maps. Let us consider, with some justifiable suspicion, the courses they recommend. The fact that they are the most promulgated and popular (and have been for several decades) almost makes them suspect at the outset, since, as I documented in the first chapter, so few people ever make it to financial freedom. The popular maps must not be living up to *their* vaunted claims.

It is worth our time to examine the strategies on some of the most common maps. It is my opinion that they include several delusive toll roads. There are six fallacies in particular I'd like you to be aware of.

FALLACY NO. 1:

A LITTLE MORE MONEY WILL SOLVE MY PROBLEMS.

The idea that more money means fewer problems is the unrivaled champion of financial fallacies. It is the most deleterious of all monetary mind sets, the most delusive, the most obstructive. It is *the* fundamental postulate in erroneous solutions to money woes, because no one gives it a second thought. It is taken as a given, "with just a little more cash, all my problems will disappear."

This myth is treacherous because it is so convenient. It does not require further thought or deeper delving. One does not have to introspect or scrutinize one's financial posture or policies. It requires no discipline or self-control, just more aggression— more (guess what) acquirement. This myth is so utilitarian. It can be employed in many ways. More money fixes *everything*. More money will solve anything from poor self-image to a rocky marriage to the daily frustrations with a dead-end job. "If I had the money, I'd tell my employer to get lost, and then I'd do something really meaningful with my life," is only one of myriad oft-uttered self-delusions. More money is the panacea which would seem to cure all ills. It is this myth upon which the "acquirement" gurus feed and get fat.

Unfortunately, more money not only does *not* solve problems, more money tends to amplify them.

I once took an informal survey of my friends and close acquaintances, who represented a broad range of occupations and lifestyles. The spectrum ranged from very modest to very high incomes. My survey consisted of two simple questions:

> (1) Do you feel you have enough money to live COMFORTABLY every month?

Take a wild stab at the predominant answer. Virtually without exception, the answer was, "NO." Most of the people in my survey, when they would be candid about it, were overspending their monthly income. For most, it was their norm.

The next question was even more revealing:

> (2) How much MORE per month would you need in order to live comfortably each month?

I was really asking them to quantify their deficit spending. Some of the people had to think about it a moment. Others had an amount or a percentage right on the tip of their tongue, which I thought was noteworthy. However, the most interesting thing of all was that a definite pattern began to appear. This verified a suspicion. When I took the additional amount that was needed to stay in the black and divided it by the monthly income, I arrived at a percentage. Plotting the responses on a chart, I began to notice that they were clustering around a specific percentage. There was some variation, but the majority fell around a significant 10 PERCENT. The mode, by a definite margin, was 10 percent.

Another interesting pattern was revealed. When there *was* spending in excess of the 10 percent figure, guess at which end of the income spectrum it occurred. Almost invariably, it was at the high income end.

In summary, the profile was this:

1. Almost everyone, high income or low, was over-spending their income.

2. The norm for overspending was 10 percent.

3. The vast majority of those who were overspending income by *greater* than 10 percent were on the high income end of the spectrum.

I found the whole portrait enlightening and it seemed to verify an economic maxim which has been kicking around for quite some time. It is called "Parkinson's Law," and states, "Spending will always rise to meet or exceed income."

The word "law" is somewhat of a misnomer here. Ordinarily, the word "law" refers to one of the inviolable principles of the universe, a basic causal reason things happen the way they happen. In the strict sense, Parkinson's Law is not a law. It can (and, in fact, *should*) be violated. However, the pattern of human behavior is so universal and consistent, one would think it was an immutable law of the galaxies.

The truth is, we are suffering from AN EPIDEMIC OF MONETARY PARKINSON'S DISEASE! The epidemic is rampant and affects us individually and collectively (or haven't you noticed the deficit spending fevers which run through Congress like an annual bout with malaria?). Individuals, families or governments who habitually deficit spend will eventually come to a day of reckoning. Choices will be limited. Opportunities will be diminished. The shackles slip on lightly and easily. Once they are in place, it requires long and concerted effort to extricate oneself and become free again.

I am tempted to launch into a harangue on governmental deficit spending, but will forebear. That will have to wait for another book. It all boils down to our own individual control and self-discipline anyway. Many of us, who would be perfectly willing to jump on the band wagon in deploring the spending habits of Congress, need to inspect our own domiciles. We cannot loudly decry deficit spending by Uncle Sam while we, ourselves, are living on our credit cards. It is hypocritical, and we know it. That is the major reason we do not, as a people, put our foot down and absolutely demand fiscal restraint by our elected leaders. Down deep we realize we are no better than they are. Can we really demand of them what we are unwilling to accomplish in our own households? No; and so we protest, but not too firmly, and government's deficit spending persists.

Getting back to the fallacy, more money is not a boon—does not solve problems—UNLESS and UNTIL something else is in place. I am convinced that, as a general rule, there is more stress and worry among my high-income friends than among those who earn less. Even if the percentage of overspending stays the same, (and in some cases it doesn't, it is higher) the actual dollar amount being spent also is obviously higher. My friends with high incomes are forging *behind* each month at a much greater pace. Some are digging a hole (how about, canyon) for themselves at breath taking rates of speed. They are heavy with debt, heavy with worry, and heavy with anxiety about the future.

I have let some of my friends of rather modest means in on this observation, and it seemed to bring them comfort in a perverse sort of way. All these years they had been harboring a fair degree of envy. It was all for naught. Their high-income friends are not the carefree, liberal spenders they appear to be. Oh, they are liberal spenders all right, but it is far from care free. Most of them toss and turn in their beds, worrying about their debts and their bills. Their debt grows annually and a lion's share of their income pours through their fingers, cascading down to their creditors. They scramble to increase their income to meet this debt service, which drives up their taxes. An accelerating, downward spiral to catastrophe becomes manifest. Incredibly, some of them compound their disastrous trends by *borrowing* to pay their *taxes*. Soon they find themselves on an incredibly merciless treadmill, and it then just becomes a question of stamina. Sooner or later they exhaust the limits of their personal machinery, start leaking oil, and burn out their pistons. Their high income has become more of a curse than a blessing.

MORE MONEY WILL *NOT* SOLVE YOUR PROBLEMS. IN MOST CASES IT ACTUALLY AMPLIFIES THEM.

Let me elucidate why. It all centers in a mind set. This mind set spawns a host of plagues and pestilences. I call it "Prospector's Mentality."

PROSPECTOR'S MENTALITY

Not far from my home in Arizona (in fact I can see it from my east windows right now) there looms an awesome geological eccentricity. It is called by the Apache Indians, "The Home of the Thunder God" and is known to almost everyone else as Superstition Mountain. It is a remarkably jagged remnant of molten matter, carved by weather into cliffs and pinnacles. Its unique, mysterious features begged to be titled, "Superstition."

Legends about this unrepeated peak abound. Perhaps you have heard of the Lost Dutchman Gold Mine. It is possible you have heard about it late at night, surrounding a campfire, where the atmosphere is conducive to the recounting of tall tales. (Phrases like "Superstition Mountain" and "Lost Dutchman" and "sacks of gold" proffer such wonderful fodder for the mind's fertile imagination.) A fabulously rich vein of gold embedded in rose quartz is supposed to be located on or near Superstition Mountain. The story has roots that go back to the 1800s.

Over the decades, thousands of hungry souls have heard the stories and come to Superstition Mountain hoping to cash in on quick riches. Each one believed he or she was something special, that the laws of the universe would make an exception, and he or she would be the one, the lucky prospector, to achieve the shortcut to the good life. For decades they have come. They still do.

Some enterprising (and more realistic) souls have even made a handsome living selling maps of the mine to the foolish. (Are you hearing the familiar echoes of Chapter 1 here?) They have mass-produced the authentic and *only* map to the mother lode by the thousands. Concocting stories about old Indians, or grizzled prospectors with death-bed confessions, they have duped the gullible into paying mind-boggling sums for totally specious maps.

The history of Superstition Mountain would almost be funny if it were not for the real tragedy it cloaks. Dozens and dozens of lives have been lost, figuratively and literally. Murders and bush-whackings still occur, even in our supposedly modern and civilized times. Literally hundreds of other lives have been squandered through the insatiable lust for prospecting.

An invariable component of the Prospector Mentality is the sense of being destiny's child. "I will be different," they say, "I can outsmart the laws of the universe. I will get rich without the trouble. The rules do not apply to me." Prospectors only outsmart themselves. They end up working anyway, but they work fruit-lessly. Hour after hour, people have toiled on the crags of this unique mountain. It has become a geological "Monument to Prospector Mentality." Infested with catclaw and cacti of every sort, this mountain has seen hundreds of people work for decades pounding on the rocks. They drill and blast, shovel and pick, haul and sift. They live in tents and sleep on the ground, believing that any moment Luck or Fate will turn their way and they will be rich. All of this stands as a great and pathetic symbol of mankind's frailties. Yet, Arizona's Superstition Mountain is not totally unique.

SAME PLOT; DIFFERENT STAGE

There are, you see, *other* monuments to Prospector Mentality. The facades are different, but the pathetic pattern is the same. The spirit of speculation is nothing more than the spirit of prospecting dressed in a business suit. The stages and scenery may vary, but the tragedy plays the same. The script unfolds like the plot in the tales of the "Lost Dutchman Mine." People hear tales of other people, sometimes friends or relatives, or friends of friend's relatives. (It doesn't really matter, you see. Avarice does not need hard facts.) The tales recount how so-and-so hit it big in penny stocks or garbanzo bean futures or raw land by an airport. Easy fortunes lie waiting to be plucked at every turn in the markets.

Prospectors believe the yarns and exaggerations without the slightest investigation and then think it is their right to also "strike it rich." So they scrape together a stake and go prospecting in the markets. When one venture comes up dry, they just try another. Sometimes they change mountains, but they never stop prospecting. They just keep promising themselves that they are different. *They* are entitled to wealth the easy way. They can, and will, circumvent the laws of accumulation. *They* will not need to follow correct principles. They are the exception in the universe.

Over the years, prospectors put in a lot of sweat and toil. As they eventually realize, prospecting is not all that easy after all. The shortcut is actually a dead end. They end up throwing their hard-earned grubstake money at the myth of quick, easy riches. In the end, most prospectors wind up paupers. No small pathos lies in the fact that if they had just kept their grubstake money and made a modest return on it, they would have lived and retired comfortably.

A LAW WITHOUT EXCEPTIONS

Now we come to a principle which, unlike Parkinson's Law, *does* hold true without exception. This concept needed a name, so I offer this one: "The Inescapable Law of Appetites, Passions and Lusts." How is that for a robustly ostentatious moniker? The Inescapable Law of Appetites, Passions and Lusts is stated simply:

SPENDING MONEY ON APPETITES, PASSIONS AND LUSTS WILL INTENSIFY THEM, RATHER THAN SATISFY THEM.

This inviolable law explains why more money is not the answer to life's dilemmas. When the sources of problems are internal, external remedies do not succeed. The truth is, unless and until the appetites, passions, and lusts are subdued, and brought into proper balance, there is *never* enough money. Reasonably ample incomes and modest investment returns are insufficient, too gradual, too plodding. To feed the appetites you have to "strike it rich—make it big and make it fast." (Prospector's Mentality is born.) To satisfy the cravings you *have* to "hit the mother lode." In order to do that, you have to go prospecting. The tried and proven methods of planting, cultivation and harvest not only lack glamour and excitement, they are, in the eyes of the prospector, "way too slow. They are for the masses of bland homesteaders and simple-minded farmers." Prospector's Mentality, full of pride, selfishness and impatience, then leads to a host of blunt disappointments. Before long, blunder after blunder ensues and the prospector becomes lost in a dry and inhospitable land of other fallacies.

CHAPTER 4

Broker Says It All

One of the most alluring fallacies on the false maps is that the rich achieved their wealth through vicarious investment.

FALLACY NO. 2:

THE RICH HAVE INVESTED THEIR WAY TO WEALTH

This obstinate myth is widely cherished. This fiction alleges that the rich achieved their wealth by eking out a small initial nest egg. They proceeded to simply relocate that modest sum in one of the lucrative markets (stock, commodity, real estate, etc.) and then, through their own astute judgments or, better yet, those of a faithful broker, struck it rich. This fantasy promptly summons Prospector's Mentality. The setting and props on the stage have changed but the plot remains the same. Take a look. If you simply change "Superstition Mountain" and call it "the markets" and substitute the word "investing for "prospecting," you have altered only the surface features. Substantially, not much has changed.

The only difference is that you add one actor or actress, who takes on the role called broker. (This player tends to be the best paid person in the cast. Later on you will see that this play only exists so that actor gets paid. The rest of the scene is secondary and is intended only to obscure that sensitive fact.) These players claim to be professional miners and mining consultants. Their tidy implication is that they are really in the know when it comes to the most lucrative veins of precious ore. They say they are there to eliminate a lot of time-consuming searching and sifting. They profess to, quickly and effectively, help the prospector locate the most promising terrain for their claims.

In real life, unfortunately, some of the respect accorded the experts is unfounded. Most prospectors would be better off if their awe was a little less generous and their regard for the "expert" advice was a little more cautious. Let us take a look at the noble performance records of the professionals to see why.

At the commencement of the 1980s, almost without exception, the pundits were predicting sky-rocketing inflation, steep interest rates, and runaway energy costs. Look it up. There was a virtual consensus on it. OPEC ruled the world, and no one would have dared utter words to the effect that inflation would suddenly come back to earth. Marching inflation was as solid as the Eastern Bloc. (Get it?) Most savants were predicting perilous times for Wall Street and the gold and silver gurus were inferring monetary collapse of the whole system.

As it turned out, you could have made an opulent fortune several times over by just selling all the experts short in the '80s. Good old inflation subsided, OPEC lost its grip on the world's throat, energy markets mimicked Humpty Dumpty, interest rates came down (many people refinanced their homes in the '80s because the interest rates were so much better than in the '70s), and there was a handsome bull market on Wall Street.

THE WOE OF TRYING TO PREDICT THE UNPREDICTABLE

I am not about to tell you that I, Dennis R. Deaton, *knew* what was going to happen. I did not know. My point is, *neither did all the "experts."* Take a look back at the Wall Street Apocalypse of the `80s—Black Monday, October 19, 1987. On Tuesday, every one of the heroic analysts and sage stock market authorities were pounding our eardrums with the forceful explanations of exactly *why* the market had taken this drastic and injurious tumble, but, there was not one of them that told you the Tuesday before that it was going to happen. That's the point. They didn't know either!

An interesting experiment in investment reality has been conducted by the Financial Traders Association (FTA). It corroborates my thesis. Since 1983, this august group has held the U.S. Trading and Investment Championships—sort of the "Olympics of Prospectors." Although it is open to anyone, it has become an arena for professional brokers to document their prowess and measure their abilities against their peers. The FTA has conducted 19 tournaments to date. Five of the 19 have been for a full year's span. All the rest have been for the much shorter time frame of four months. The rationale is that the four-month span is the best indication of a trader's real ability to pick fast-rising winners (to find the best veins of ore the quickest).

The scoreboard tells volumes. Out of 3500 entrants only 22 percent wound up with even a modest profit! These are the *pros*! In baseball, that is a batting average of .220. You don't make the Hall of Fame with that. In 1989, the Detroit Tigers, the worst team in baseball, who lost over 100 games, at least hit .242!

Let me also remind you that these FTA investment contests have been conducted over a period of time which has been described, overall, as one of the finest bull markets in U.S. history. It is a good thing the general market trends were strongly upward or there is no telling what embarrassment would have occurred.

One can hardly argue with Paul Harwitz's quip: "We wouldn't be any worse off if we let the economists predict the weather and the meteorologists predict the economy."

The vast majority of financial advisers and brokers make far more money from commissions on your transactions than from their own brilliant investments. Do you think they would spend all their time on the phone, dialing for dollars, if they were making it hand over fist in their own portfolios? They make money from managing transactions, not miracles.

If you are still wavering a bit, finding it hard to think knowledgeable players do not launch yachts every day through their own piercing insights into the markets, ask yourself why Ivan Boesky (among many others) has to cheat to get rich. Without the illegal advantage of inside knowledge, it is, at best, just a game of craps for them, too.

This holds true with all the prognostication magi. Examine their batting averages, and you will see that the vast majority of them could not make your child's Little League team. Check it out yourself, and have some fun and laughs doing it. Go to your library and check out all of the prognosticatory economic texts of the '70s—the ones with the apocalyptic titles—and read them. Do the same with the books of the '80s. With the clear advantage of perfect hindsight, you will plainly see that the financial emperors have no clothes.

I do not have an old ax to grind here. I have not had a "bad experience" in the stock market. I am not engaging in broker-bashing because I want to get even for alleged injustices in my past. I have never lost money in the stock market. This is primarily due to the fact that I have never *played* (note the verb) the stock market. In fact, I have several friends who are stock brokers. We are friends principally because I do *not* use their services. They do not need to be embarrassed around me and I do not have to fight off any ill feelings towards them. It is the only smart thing to do.

One of my friends works in a large brokerage with a well-known name. (If I were to mention it, you would surely recognize it.) There are dozens of brokers in his office. One day I asked my friend, "How many of your colleagues made money on their *own* stock portfolio last year?"

He responded, "Well, I don't know. But it would be interesting to know."

I said, "Wouldn't it? Why don't you take a little survey and ask them?" Guess what? He did, and not one—NOT ONE—of them had made a profit on their *own* portfolio that year. Only two claimed to have made even a slight profit in the previous *two* years. It was difficult to look beyond that; the turnover was so great, very few of the brokers had been there long enough to extend the survey. Many of the brokers he had worked with five years previous were in other lines of work. That also tells you something.

I offer one hypothesis: Eventually the integrity issue gets to them. As I stated earlier, brokers are not crooks. They are sincerely trying to do their best. Sooner or later, a lot of them realize that they are sitting ducks. They cannot win. Time and the unpredictability of the world are against them. No matter what they say, they step on their tongues. In fact, the only way they could consistently break even is if they mathematically divided their advice on a strict 50-50 basis. Every time they told Mrs. X that stock ABC was going to go up, they would immediately tell Mrs. Y that the very same stock was going to go down. That way they would always break even. Well, not *always*, because every once in a while a stock might not move up or down—just stay right where it is. Then they would have misinformed both Mrs. X and Mrs. Y.

They have a tough life. They cannot win. My heart goes out to them; and my advice to you is befriend them, console them, but, whatever you do, DON'T GO PROSPECTING WITH THEM. They don't *know* where the Lost Dutchman Mine is any better than you do.

What is true of the stock market, holds true in the other financial arenas as well. There are "new and improved" soothsayers everywhere. The theatre is different, but the play is the same. Unpredictability. Sooner or later, it gets them all.

WHO'S FAULT IS IT?

Economists, market analysts and brokers do not have extra-sensory powers. (Most don't even claim such. It is we, in our greed, who wish they did.) Regardless of what we may think, they are not even more innately brilliant than we. In fact the evidence suggests they might be less—after all, they have gotten themselves trapped in a no-win situation.

There is no way financial forecasters can be consistently correct. One cannot predict the unpredictable. They don't know because it is *impossible* to know. They are prospecting, too. They are picking around, sifting the dirt, trying to stumble onto a nugget now and then; and now and then they do, but *mostly* they do not. You see, they are real human beings, too. They are not messiahs. Most are just conscientious men and women with families to support just like you and me.

Some of them (unwisely) *try* to play the part of omniscient savants of the East, but it is actually our *own* weakness which is being exploited here. THE SELF-SAME PEOPLE WHO WILL LOOK YOU SINCERELY IN THE EYE AND AVER, "THERE IS NO SUCH THING AS A FREE LUNCH," ARE THE VERY ONES WHO TURN RIGHT AROUND AND EXPECT A BROKER TO MAKE THEM RICH. A little consistency here would work wonders.

Those who attempt the role of Impeccable Prophet go on for years "getting away with it," because there are thousands of us who subconsciously wish that they *were* infallibly wise and *could* forecast the future. The fact is, they would not be able to get away with it if we did not let them. The only difference between Johnny Carson's "Karnak the Magnificent" (whom I love) and these other mystics is that Karnak does not begin to take himself seriously. We recognize that the whole thing is a farce from the outset. With the "mystics of the markets" it is also a farce, but *we* don't want to admit it. When their turbans slip, we pretend not to see. We keep playing along, hoping that these vaudevillian players can serve us free lunch. Actually, they don't even serve refreshments.

A personal integrity check is in order here. Many of us will shake our fists at the brokers, and phone our attorneys demanding vile retribution, when they fail to produce the jewels and baubles we request, but whose fault *is* this? Who is really kidding who here? It is we who are kidding ourselves.

And, if you think the answer is to just go it alone, to play the market without their expert advice, you still have not gotten the point. With or without a consulting adviser, you are still prospecting. If you think you are the one chosen individual in the universe who can make a living *and* concurrently (without a guru's help) invest and successfully manage your investments (most prospectors are loners anyway), please be aware that the odds are not in your favor, either. Speculative investment is anything but the sure way to ample riches.

The findings of a study funded in part by the National Science Foundation reveal information to further substantiate this thesis. Interviews were conducted of a large sample of "self-made" millionaires. These were individuals who had not inherited wealth, but had achieved it through their own efforts.

One of the interesting common denominators of this group was that they were NOT crafty investors. They did not, as the myth suggests, take a grubstake and relentlessly invest their way to wealth. How they obtained their wealth will be dealt with later, but it was *not* through speculation.

To further emphasize the point, when these individuals did get around to putting some of their money into speculative markets, they fared no better than the rank and file of the earth (or better than the pros in the FTA example). Making their fortunes elsewhere, some of them put money into "investment markets" and seldom made that money grow. The norm was, they, too, lost cash.

THE "BUT WHAT ABOUT..." SYNDROME

On one occasion, in a seminar I was conducting, I was challenged by a gentleman. He contended that it was possible to get rich through investment. First, let me clarify that I am not saying that you *can* not. I am saying that you *will* not. I am not trying to play cutesy with you here. I am trying to make a point. There does, theoretically, exist a possibility that you *can* get rich through investment, but it is highly unlikely that you will. The odds are just not in your favor. It is like the lottery. Yes, *somebody* does win the lottery, but the statistical reality is, it *won't be you*. The likelihood is so remote that if you are betting your future on the lottery, you are going to have to get used to a long stretch of disappointment.

Anyway, back to the story. I was challenged by a gentleman who said he was *personally* acquainted with a man who had made excellent gains in real estate investment. He told the story in some detail. His friend had bought low and sold high, deal after deal, and had arrived on easy street by wheeling and dealing in real estate.

I asked the question, "Did your friend ever lose any money at all on real estate? Did every deal wind up making him money?" The honest answer was, "I don't know." I offered this thought, "Sure, we all have heard of people making a sweet deal or two, but the question is how well they have done *overall*. Net. What is the picture when all ventures are summed? My father made a handsome profit on Western Airlines stock when they merged with Delta, but if you take his total stock market experience he has wound up with a modest loss, all things considered." The man in my seminar said, to be fair, he would check it out and let me know.

True to his word, he did just that. A few weeks after the seminar, I received a call. He reported that we were both right. I wasn't sure how that could be since we were seemingly on opposite sides of table. He said, up to the point in his friend's life that was being cited at the seminar, this friend had never gone anywhere but up. He had entered into four real estate transactions and each one had gone well. He had made money each time. In fact, each succeeding deal had been a little bigger and a little better, because he was reinvesting his profits (winnings) from the preceding venture. That was the point in the history when the man from my seminar had lost contact with his real estate investor friend, and the two had not been in close contact for a couple of years. He had been right, he emphasized; his friend had made good money investing.

"But," he said (I had been waiting for that word for a couple of minutes), now it was my turn to be right. His friend had rolled the majority of his profits (keep reading, winnings) into one more venture. He had leveraged a very large apartment complex and had lost everything. The bottom fell out of the rental market (unexpectedly, of course). No one would have dreamed it (of course), and he had hung on for a while trying to weather the storm, but the downturn outlasted his cash flow and he lost it all. A significant quotation was passed on to me then, second-hand from this investor. It is deadly accurate. The investor had said to his friend, "When it comes to real estate, it's only your latest deal that really counts."

The gentleman from the seminar went on to say, "You see, you *can* so get rich in real estate." I questioned him, as I wanted to see clearly how he thought the foregoing was a success story. He countered my probings with, "Well, my friend was doing great until this last deal. *I* would have had the good sense to quit while I was ahead." Right! Classic Prospector's Mentality.

THE DIFFERENCE IS A MIND SET

There are two distinct mind sets in the world of money. One leads to prosperity and peace of mind. The other leads to frustration, disappointment and a hunger which cannot be satisfied. Take a guess at which of the two is which:

> (1) "I am the exception in the universe. The laws, which apply to everyone else, do not apply to me."

> (2) "I am not an exception. I must apply correct principles in order to obtain the benefits I seek."

Prospector's Mentality is a self-imposed delusion. It does not listen to reason or judgment. The more you cater to it, the more powerful it grows. Strike it rich or strike it poor, underlying it all is uncontrolled, mortal passion. Those who finally hit a vein now and then are unable to hang on to it, because they have never conquered that passion. Lacking personal discipline and self-control, Prospector's Mentality drives them to further speculation. The hunger is not satiated by the riches, it is actually augmented by them. They think they can do it one more time—this time REALLY big—and sooner or later they "crap out" and they are back to prospecting again.

The people who have made big money in the land bonanzas (*and have kept it*) were not really prospecting in the first place. They were sort of accidental investors. They were miraculously patient, holding onto their property as it marched higher and higher in value, because buying low and selling high was the furthest thing from their mind. They were "homesteaders" not prospectors. The passions are entirely different. They had bought a piece of property for entirely different motives and were actually quite surprised when someone came up to them and offered huge sums of money to buy their "homestead." Most of them had to do a lot of soul-searching before they could actually bring themselves to part with their possession. Good old prospectors, on the other hand, cannot wait to cash in their strike so they can get to the saloon and begin their carousing and riotous living.

CHAPTER 5

Risky Business

The bottom line in so many acquirement books is, "If you are not risking a bundle, you are a dolt." The writers of such maps do not come right out and phrase it that bluntly. (That is not the way you sell a product.) But their attitude is plain. They glorify risk. They extol opportunism. They sneer at conservatism. They guffaw at thrift. It is an age-old tactic: "If the evidence is not on your side, use ridicule." It is such a handy technique because you can eschew lengthy, time-consuming facts and explanations. Scorn is brief. You can dismiss your victim in a haughty hurry.

THE ONE-MINUTE MILLIONAIRE

Due to my far-flung speaking schedule, I get to spend some time in airports. When I have a few minutes to pass, I find myself gravitating to the bookstores, and one of my favorite pastimes is to browse through the personal finance section. I love to admire the tomes on what I call, "THE ONE-MINUTE MIL-LIONAIRE SHELF." You know the ones I mean—the ones with the glitzy, enticing titles that appeal to our passions: *How To Make A Fortune In Termite Futures, How To Profit From The Next Solar Eclipse, How To Start A Billion Dollar Aerospace Business*

In Your Basement With Nothing Down. (I can hardly keep from drooling.)

It reminds me of when I was a boy and went to the barber shop. There was a certain magazine there: "Argosy." (I think it was a law that it only be disseminated to barber shops.) In the back of the magazine there were always beguiling advertisements which ran something like this: "Draw this Pirate and Have an Exciting Career in Neurosurgery." The ad would go on to say that neurosurgeons were just ordinary folks like you and me, who had developed a knack for artistic dexterity, which any of us could learn—on our own—at home—in our spare time—with the help of this one simple and *inexpensive* HOME CORRESPONDENCE COURSE. Ah yes, the path to the operating room made simple and easy. The hook line, "Earn money in your spare time, without leaving home," still rings nostalgically in my ears.

Somehow, however, even as a boy, that type of come-on seemed wormy to me. I have not seen "Argosy" magazine lately, but I still see the come-ons in one form or another. Some of them are actually quite sophisticated. You do not even have to draw the pirate any more. And, they are longer now—more lengthy than magazine ads. Some are book length. (Don't be fooled by their length. They are still come-ons.) GRQ (Get Rich Quick) Books we'll call them. The GRQ Books abound and sell millions of copies annually. But heed one warning: In general, when it comes to texts on financial advice, the older they are the better.

Do not be misled by the GRQ Books. Do not let your greed or your glands get the better of you. Such tendencies cause impatience and impetuousness. These are not qualities which beget wealth.

Grandpa said it often, and it still applies—"Ain't no such thing as instant crops." Patience and sound judgement are qualities of the financially free.

Grandpa would counsel us to keep hoeing while others throw their caution (and seeds) to the wind believing:

FALLACY NO. 3:

YOU CAN'T GET RICH ON SAFE INVESTMENTS

The GRQ Books are false maps. They prey on greed and impatience. The false map makers love to extol the virtues of risk. It is the *fast* way to riches. It is *simple*. It is *smart*. (Ah yes, just my kind of map: Fast. Simple. Shrewd.)

As if the "you can get rich quick in your spare time with nothing down" ploy were not enough, they distort the picture even further by attempting to say theirs is the *only* game in town. Without the slightest compunction, they assert that you and I will *never* succeed by taking a safe, conservative approach. We will need to speculate, live life on the edge, and cash in on some *really* big scores. If we don't (quick Virginia, grab the children) the "Big Bad Wolf" (alias, Inflation) will blow our house down and eat up our conservative little nest eggs and we will not be able to afford even the bare necessities when we retire. Our buying power will be "all swallowed up" by the Big Bad Wolf.

As I proceed to offer you a few classic examples of this rhetoric, let me also offer you a very important idea: Creative genius, which is predicated on focus, and which flourishes when preoccupations and distractions are at a minimum, is the greatest source of wealth. Your own creative enterprise is more likely to make you wealthy than any speculative venture you will ever undertake.

Anything which detracts from focus and clear, calm thinking is an antagonist of the first order. It will work against you as you confront and deal with the wolf.

With that as a backdrop, let me quote from a book titled *The Zurich Axioms* by Max Gunther. One cannot help but admire

Mr. Gunther's choice of titles—how deftly it conveys unquestion-
able authority. It is so replete with innuendos and connotations of
authenticity, one cannot help but be enticed by it. "Zurich"—
connotes solid, engorged Swiss Bank Accounts brimming with
bundles of money from all sectors of the world. "Axioms"—no
hypotheses here—just fool-proof mathematical statements of
immutable truths of the cosmos—infallible formulae—the tried
and proven equations that guarantee the brimming vaults. Even
"The" is a bull's eye. (I did say, *eye.*) "The"—not "a partial list
of" or "a few" or even "some." No, it is "*THE*" Zurich Axioms!
Well done, Max.

    In the very first chapter of the book, on the very first page
(yep, page 1), the very first statement reads, "Worry is not a
sickness but a sign of health. If you are not worried, you are not
risking enough." Makes me sleep better already. How about you?

    Another book (and friend, if you ever get a chance to read
this one, pass it up!) is *The Omega Strategy* by William D.
Montapert. This pseudo-sophisticated title is a real eye-catcher.
Sounds like one of those intrigue novels by Robert Ludlum. (And,
why not? Fiction is fiction, right?) Anyway, the subtitle is what
I want you to contemplate: "How You Can Retire Rich by the End
of the Eighties." Looking back, we have the advantage of seeing
how accurate the book really was.

    First of all, the major premise: the economy is going to go
into a deflation cycle, short but pronounced. This will be followed
by one last hyper-inflated surge, and then everything is going to
come to an abysmal crash. Naturally, you and I have only one sure
way out of all of this—Mr. Montapert's book. It is our *only* hope.

    Quoting directly from the opening paragraphs:

> Once in a lifetime there comes a period of economic
> change so disruptive that those with very little money can
> seize the opportunity to become rich, while the very rich,
> seemingly protected by conservative investments, can be
> reduced to near poverty almost overnight. *Such a time is now
> at hand.* Here is the strategy.

Looking at this statement from today's perspective, there is only one thing to say, "Ooooops."

I am sure if the author were here to defend his position, he would say that his theory is not incorrect, just his sense of timing. "It is sure to happen. It just did not happen in the '80s. It looks very probable that it will now be more like the '90s." This is the stock answer. Our magi friends feel totally justified in telling us that one day they will be right, while ignoring the reality, that every other day of our lives they are patently wrong. I just can not find it in my heart to be impressed with someone who has predicted 99 of the last two catastrophes.

Permit me to extend this little foray a bit further. (We *are* having fun, aren't we?) It is not that I want to ruin anyone's day, I simply want to impress upon your mind that risk is a tenuous strategy, that the false map makers are not to be heeded without caution and that, when they tell you risk is the *only* avenue open to you, they are flatly wrong.

On the back cover, to sell his book, Mr. Montapert's publisher tells us what we are about to gain for our effort:

> Learn: why experts think speculating is the safest way to make money at this time. Why you and even the rich can't depend on cash, money market funds, Keogh and IRA plans, and other "safe" investments. How to pinpoint the end of the current deflation and make a killing when inflation zooms again...

Again, all of this was to transpire in the '80s. Now, I am on the road quite a bit, it must have happened while I was out of town. I seem to have missed it.

At least he is forthright enough to title his book accurately, *The Omega Strategy*. Omega is the last letter in the Greek alphabet, and anyone who followed this strategy in the '80s wound up in last place, too!

DIFFERENT TYPES OF RISK

Now, back to reality. RISK IS RISK. It is simply that. It is not inherently wicked, bad, nasty, crude, rude, lewd, socially unacceptable, coarse, common or cheap. BUT! NEITHER IS IT THE AUTOMATIC "PATH OF GLORY" LEADING TO UN-TOLD RICHES. The false map makers tell you that it was the risk takers who have made America great, that risk takers are the ones who have caused civilization to advance out of the Stone Age. They ask us to just think where we'd all be if Columbus, Joan of Arc, George Washington, and the Little Rascals had not risked their all for the good of mankind. They want to make you feel like you are a moral wimp if you are not down in the arenas of speculation, gladiating with the lions.

But hold on there, pardner ... that is just the point. Let's not mix apples and oranges here. Just what kind of moral fiber are we talking about, anyway? The fiber of discipline, or the fiber of avarice?

There is a VAST difference between having an ideal which you firmly and resolutely believe in, and, while maintaining *direct* control, are willing to risk your life, your fortune and your sacred honor for—a big difference between *that* and the notion of flinging your money into the hands of the money-changers and politely asking them to call you when you are rich!

Let me make it clear: I am not categorically adverse to risk. Like everything else, risk comes in grades and degrees. Even well-planned investments and enterprises contain an element of risk, and I accept that. Life offers no perfect, flawless guarantees. Philosophically, there is an element of risk in everything we do. But, I emphatically dislike what the false map makers do with that philosophical window. Extolling risk practically for its own sake, they remind us (as though it was some profound insight) that, "Just getting into a car and driving to the grocery store is a risk." Philosophically, yes. Realistically, no. Practically speaking, the risk, for the average, prudent person, of driving to the store is so infinitesimally small, it is not truly a life threatening experience. (In the case of the grocery store, the risk comes *after* one gets there.)

What I am opposed to is the persistent assertion of the GRQ artists that speculation is not only the best way, but the *only* way to wealth. There is nothing innately magical about risk, in and of itself. Contrary to what the GRQ books would imply, the words "investment" and "risk" are not automatically synonymous terms. Nor are "investment" and "reasonable safety" mutually exclusive. The map makers dramatically distort the picture. I contend that prudent moves can be made which will bring solid, real and more-than-adequate returns without this arrogant, quasi-Kamikaze approach so ballyhooed. Their definition of risk is merely a cheap euphemism for profligate gambling.

It did not take long for Blackie Sherrod, a nationally known columnist, to see through the ruse, either. Years ago he quipped:

> If you bet on a horse, that's gambling. If you bet you can make three spades, that's entertainment. If you bet cotton will go up three points, that's business. See the difference?

The fallacy occurs when the so-called financial authorities tell you that *high* risk is THE ONLY WAY to attain ample wealth. I whole-heartedly disagree. There is a safe, sure way to financial peace of mind, and acquirement-minded speculation is antithetic to it.

THE ALL-IMPORTANT RETURN

High risk puts cash in jeopardy. Sometimes you win. Sometimes you lose. When losses occur, statistics show that extraordinary earnings are required thereafter, to just make up for that loss, let alone what could have been a modest growth on that vanished sum. In the vast majority of cases, people who lose large chucks are never able to make it up and would have been so much better off if they'd just conserved their principal, with a modest gain on it, in the first place.

Nine times out of ten, when losses do occur, it is because the "investor" was more concerned with the rate of return than with the likelihood of return. The first priority should always be the conservation of the original sum—the principal. Generally when conservation becomes secondary to the rate of return, it is a cardinal sign that the message of Chapter 2 has been forgotten. Acquirement has supplanted accumulation as the central mind set. Maintaining a firm hold on the fundamental perspective of accumulation prevents a multitude of errors and regrets. Remember Accumulation Law No. 2, "Don't Lose What You Save."

In the United States, we could practically retire the national debt on the principal alone, never mind the promised fabulous rates of return, which has been lost through speculation over the past two decades by hard-working men and women in this country.

The Better Business Bureau, in a report published in February of 1988, estimates that the losses to outright fraudulent entities amounts to $40 BILLION a year! Add to that the losses in the so-called legitimate vehicles and the figures are staggering.

The toughest question in monetary matters is how much risk is *too* much. There are no pat answers or formulas. One thing is certain, however. Those who forget that preserving the principal is the first priority will often let greed overrule sound judgment. Overly increasing the risk factor in order to enhance the growth factor is unwise strategy. Rates of return which are "too good to be true," are exactly that. You have heard that a million times; heed it.

I distinctly recall a television ad which ran prominently in my state a few years ago. It was for an organization which called itself "Investors Clearing House" It promised annual returns of 24 percent. At the time I told my wife to make a mental note, that we would be hearing sad news about ICH in the future. My gut feeling proved to be correct. Within the year the news media were running stories about how Investors Clearing House had "cleaned house" on hundreds of imprudent "investors." These poor (literally) souls had taken their funds out of conservative vehicles, enticed by the glitter of these phenomenal "rates of return." They paid dearly for their impatience. Many lost their life's savings.

REMEMBER, THE RETURN *OF* YOUR PRINCIPAL IS MUCH MORE IMPORTANT THAN RETURN *ON* YOUR PRINCIPAL.

I have never quite understood how taking large risks with our money keeps the Big Bad Wolf of Inflation away from our doors anyway. I fail to see any *automatic* connection there. Whether I go prospecting in the markets or not inflation will be there.

The false map makers always seem to want to give credence to their postulates by referring to potential ravages of inflation. They always want to ask me where I will be if the Big Bad Wolf of Inflation comes out of the woods and rants around the economy at double or triple digits. "How, Dr. Deaton, will you fare then with your conservative little basket of investments?" My answer to them is simple: I will be a heck of a lot better off with my principal and modest increase if the Big Bad Wolf wreaks havoc than I would be if I *don't* have my principal or *any* increase.

I would much rather have my principal with a modest gain, whether nasty old inflation goes to triple digits or not, than have the empty promises of stunning returns which result, instead, in the loss of my whole wallet.

Let me make one more thing clear, so there is no misunderstanding. Yes, inflation is real. Yes, inflation does erode purchasing power—does shrink the dollar—does plunder the eggs. I am not denying the existence of inflation, nor its potential harms. Ultimately, however, it all comes down to volume. The more dollars you have, the better off you are going to be, regardless of inflation's fevers and remissions. THE BEST HEDGE AGAINST INFLATION STARTS WITH *NOT* LOS-ING A FORTUNE.

By the way, even my four-year-old, Emily, can tell you that the little pig which fared the best, after all, was the one who built his house solidly and surely, brick by brick, and wasn't in a hurry to dance and play all day.

CHAPTER 6

Prison Terms

About the only thing worse than losing a fortune is going to prison. In prison your time is not your own; your opportunities and options are confiscated or at least severely limited. You accumulate no fortunes. You waste your time, your talents—your life.

Debt is prison. I did not invent that metaphor, it literally has been around for centuries. You have heard it before. You are going to hear it again. There is a reason for that. Bondage and prison are still, by far, the most accurate and appropriate metaphors to describe the consequences of debt. The fact that the metaphor is so well known makes it all the more poignant. Somehow the message does not seem to sink in. People keep applying their own handcuffs. They lock themselves in the prison of debt (and throw away the key) with alarming frequency. Sadly, the rate of occurrence is actually on the increase.

U.S. government statistics at the close of 1990 reported personal bankruptcies were on the rise, right along with credit buying. Consumer debt (not for major acquisitions like houses and cars, but consumptive "credit card" debt) doubled in the decade of the `80s. In that 10-year period there was a major leap in credit addiction and the willful acceptance of the shackles of deficit spending.

More will be said later about the effects of installment buying and the impact that it has on a personal estate. This chapter, instead, will undertake the subject of debt from another perspective and will discuss two other rude forms of debt incarceration. The false map makers lead you to believe that debt is a thoroughfare to riches. That is Fallacy No. 4.

FALLACY NO. 4:

THE ROAD TO FINANCIAL FREEDOM IS PAVED WITH DEBT.

Can you imagine walking into a bank and saying, "Hello, I want to borrow just enough money to get out of debt?" Robert G. Allen, well-known author, says you can do just that. He has written two best sellers on leverage in real estate. On page 16 of his book, *Creating Wealth*, (this is obviously a typo; he must have meant *Creating Welts*) we read, "In fact, self-made wealth never comes without going into debt." Come on, Robert, NEVER? He continues:

> I repeat: You can never become wealthy without going into some form of investment debt. And probably a lot of it....You can actually borrow your way to wealth.

Not quite. There is one *very* important step after the borrowing that is really the crux of the matter. Before I point that out, let me make sure some terms are understood. The tactic of speculating in real estate (or other commodities) with little or no money down is called "leverage." The leverage technique is employed to gain control of some item with as little money up front as possible. In exchange for control, with little or nothing down, you offer to pay for the item, usually with interest, at some later date. The thinking is that you may be able to sell the item at a higher price than you agreed to pay, before the repayment costs start eating you alive. If you are able to sell the leveraged property high enough and/or early enough (a big if), you stand to make a profit. It is, in summary, an attempt to make a profit with timing and bravado. Instead of using your money, you are using, instead, your credit and the supposed power of "borrowed" funds.

Those who advocate leverage strategies start with the basic assumption that the smartest thing one could ever do is to work on OPM (Other People's Money). This technique has gained wide popularity over the years, although its track record is wholly unimpressive. This stratagem, like many popular fads, finds favor in the hearts of the masses because it appeals strongly to human lusts. The implicit premise seems to be that one may acquire handsome profits while omitting the drudgery of first accumulating a little money to work with. For those with the "acquirement only" mind set, the glands shift into overdrive, because it appears they can immediately leap from poverty to wealth in one easy step, called "borrowing." Good old greed steps in here, and they start breathing heavy, thinking they are about to be wealthy without all the menial labor.

There is a certain air of arrogance present with most of the superstars of the leverage game. They smugly rely on the supposition that *they* are smarter than the folks from whom they are borrowing the funds. They make the assumption that the OP with the M in the first place are totally oblivious to great ways of making money, that the lenders have no idea in the world what the leveragers are up to, and that the lenders have no clue whatsoever as to what a superior strategy might be. (Sometimes letting another guy swim with a hundred pound millstone around his neck, for nothing down, isn't the dumbest thing OP might do.)

Somehow my observation has been otherwise. I have come to the conclusion that the OP who have M in the first place know something that the P without M don't. (It sort of explains why OP have all that M to begin with.) The basic assumption, that one guy is so much smarter than the other guy, tends to produce debacles, rather than delights. It has something to do with "pride going before a fall," or something along those lines.

Anyway, there is your short course in definitions. You now know what "leverage" means and what "OPM" means. (You also have received, free of charge, a timely editorial on the same.)

Now, back to what is so misleading about the idea that you can actually borrow your way to wealth. It implies that the brilliant key is the *borrowing*. That is not the case. The borrowing is easy. That is why people jump on this band wagon with such glee. Borrowing is easy. They have done it before, and they are good at it.

However, once the property is leveraged, people wake up to the real crux of the nothing-down game. The hard part is not getting control of the property, the kicker is getting *OUT OF CONTROL* of the property—especially with any kind of a profit. The real art is the cunning to be able to *sell* that little piece of turf for *MORE* than what you tied it up for...*PLUS* the interest you paid...*PLUS* the taxes, insurance, maintenance and repair costs, lawyer's fees (to evict the *&%#$ deadbeats who would not be so kind as to pay their rents)...*PLUS* the advertising costs to run the rental ads, and then, eventually, to run a "For Sale By Owner, Nothing Down Required" ad. (Get my drift?) I contend if you are *that* good of a salesperson you do not need to leverage to make a handsome fortune, anyway. (I will gladly accept your resume and pay you handsome commissions to sell stuff I no longer want.)

What really bothers me about the leverage gang is that they emphasize the acquirement aspects, as if that were some difficult art, while giving scant and feeble warnings of the myriad pitfalls inherent in real estate ownership and management. They glibly tell you to "buy low and, one year later, sell high," offering only slight reference to the abundant risks involved. They seldom tender so much as an anemic paragraph, explaining, for example, how to dispose of the stuff when it marches down in value, or how to extricate oneself from a negative cash flow and pay back the leveraged principle with interest when one is unable to sell the property in 12 months. They only paint a small portion of the picture, and the whole premise is highly suspect.

Albert Lowry is a classic example. Mr. Lowry authored a book, published in 1977, titled, *How You Can Become Financially Independent by Investing in Real Estate*. By 1979, it was a best-seller. His catchy hook line, "Give me only one hour a day and you can retire in three years," packed people into his seminars. At $495 per pupil, his seminars typically grossed from $100,000 to $200,000 per weekend in the large metropolitan areas. Lowry, a classic acquirement-minded prospector, seemed to have hit the mother lode.

However, life is a marathon, not a 50-yard-dash. The celebration of quick riches did not go the distance. The "father of leveraged real estate" began hitting hard times by the mid-1980s, as his wonderful little chunks of real estate became cement running shoes. Lowry stumbled and fell face down on the track as one of his real estate ventures near Lake Tahoe became not only a fiasco, but a lesson in real estate reality. In May, 1987, one short decade after the publishing of his run away best-seller, he filed for bankruptcy. Not many of his students sent sympathy cards, they were mired in financial quagmires of their own.

Methods employed by the leverage enthusiasts do not work long-term, nor most of the time, nor in most areas of the country (in general, real estate nationwide is not soaring to nose-bleed heights at high G-force rates), nor over the broad spectrum of the economy, nor for the vast majority of people. The parameters are strait; and, far too many people end up borrowing their way to bondage, instead of wealth. These "leverage giants" do not make the *spendable* wealth they imply, year in and year out, nor have they amassed sizeable liquid fortunes by such means to see themselves through the long haul. Here and there they can cite a successful example, but they never let you in on the whole picture—the net, liquid gain from *all* their leveraging contortions.

Overall, their financial pathways are not Zurich-vault material, and they are dealing you only partial truths at best.

One of Albert Lowry's former partners became persona non grata by blatantly displaying the dirty wash: "I don't know any of them who made a fortune in real estate, either before they started teaching or since."

It does not take an Einstein to run out and buy a lot of real estate with nothing down, record it on a personal financial statement, over-estimate its market value, and appear to gain substantial net worth on paper.

That it's all on paper is precisely the point. People who play the leverage game always (and only) talk about how much they are worth. They cannot talk about how much they *have*—in the bank, liquid and spendable. Their "wealth" is all on paper. Instead of counting actual dollars in hand, those who play the "Leverage a Great Net Worth" game talk about how much they are worth when they subtract (on paper) their liabilities from their "assets." Simultaneously, they speak of selling their choice little properties for exactly what they have written on the paper as though it were as easy as cracking an egg. You see, *"there's* the rub." They receive their session in reality therapy when they go to "cash in" their tidy holdings.

You can borrow your way to wealth only if you can actually convert the leveraged properties into spendable *cash* over and above all the drain. Once in a great while, it can be done. But, remember, remember, the oldest adage in the market: 'TIS MUCH EASIER TO *BUY*, THAN TO SELL. That caveat is especially true when it comes to real estate. It is, by far, *the most illiquid* investment vehicle of them all. You must find some one gullible enough to pay you more than you paid for it—not just the purchase price—*all* you paid for it. In addition, you must find not just any gullible person, you have got to find a gullible person *with loads of liquid cash* to gleefully fork over. That narrows the market considerably. You just do not find fabulously rich people *THAT* gullible on every corner.

That is why leverage is a trap. And, that is why it is such an illiquid game. You cannot get cashed out of your rentals, so you, too, must offer terms. It is not all that difficult to buy rentals with nothing down, because that is about the only way people with a lot of dumpy real estate can unload it!

Most people who play the leverage game come to rue it like no other mistake in their life. They find that their "net worth games" were self-delusions and what they were worth on paper and what they can convert to cash are two entirely different sums.

These people also discover that you have to work harder than an oarsman—toiling, sweating and struggling—putting in incredible hours in order to go broke in real estate. In some investment vehicles you can go broke in one morning. Like the commodities market—slam, bam, zap—in just a couple of hours you are wiped out. You are busted before you know what hits you. You are broke, but you still have your health and strength.

Not so in real estate. You have got to *work* at going broke. You have got to clean it, rent it, pay taxes on it, repair it, maintain it, insure it, re-rent it, re-repair it—you must keep throwing money here and money there after it. *Gradually*, after hundreds of hours, and back-breaking labor, and worry, and fuss, and pain and mental, physical and emotional anguish...you go broke. That is the beauty of the leverage strategy—you create *welts*, not wealth. You are so covered with contusions and lacerations from the blows you have endured by being a landlord, you look like you barely survived a street fight.

If you follow the advice of the OPM experts and leverage at least two rental properties a year, in no time at all, a street fight will seem mild by comparison. You will come to a salient insight: You will see clearly the two happiest days of your life—(1) the day you bought some apartments, and (2) the day you dumped those (blankety-blank) apartments.

You do not have to take my word for it. Talk to people who have played the leverage game, and 95 percent of them will tell you that if they had just put all the money they spent in interest, and repairs, and insurance, and so forth, in the bank and gotten four percent on it, they would have been light-years ahead on their journey to financial freedom. Add to that the price they have paid in mental distractions and emotional wear-and-tear, and you start to see why so many of the leverage boys are wearing toupees.

There are not two people in a hundred that would do it again, or would have gotten into leveraged real estate in the first place, had they known *all* the costs. For them, THE ROAD TO FINANCIAL FREEDOM WAS NOT PAVED WITH DEBT.

EXPOSITORY NOTES

NOTE NO. 1 - I AM NOT CATEGORICALLY DENI-GRATING REAL ESTATE AS AN INVESTMENT VEHICLE. I *am* adamantly condemning a specific *category* of real estate investment—*leveraged* real estate. It is the indebtedness aspects which you must avoid with a vengeance.

NOTE NO. 2 - WHEN ENTERING INTO ANY IN-VESTMENT, COUNT ALL THE COSTS—NOT JUST THE HARD DOLLAR COSTS—BUT *ALL* THE COSTS. There are subtle, but real, payments that you make as an investor. How much time and attention (mind power!) will be required to preserve the viability of the investment must be carefully weighed. In the long run, that is the single biggest issue in the whole game of life. How does it force you to spend *your time*, and how much time, and how much is that worth in the full perspective?

NOTE NO. 3 - DEBT IS A MENTAL DISTRACTION OF THE FIRST ORDER. For every pound of debt you carry, you are paying a price in preoccupation and dissipated power of the mind. True, some handle debt differently ("better" is a value judgment) than others, but any way you look at it, your mind is diverted to the "care of your goods" and away from higher priorities.

Please recall my physician friend noted in Chapter 2. The biggest mistake he made was when he started to "invest" in order to get out of debt! He confused two completely separate issues. Had he, first, retired a large part of his debt, his ventures would not have pressured his cash flow so drastically. Nor would the combination of the pressure and distraction have deflected him from his highest priority, the care of the patients in his practice. Ultimately that was his undoing.

NOTE NO. 4 - DEBT DRIVES UP COSTS, REDUCING PROFITS. My very good friend and partner, Reece Bawden, was once an owner-broker of a successful Century-21 Real Estate firm. He saw Note No. 4 in action time and time again in the real estate business. Someone would buy a piece of property with a low down payment and pay interest on the contract. Some even borrowed the down payment and added that interest expense to the debit side of the ledger. Their property, in most cases, did appreciate, but not enough to off-set the monthly ticking on the interest meter.

Think about it. That piece of property has got to appreciate at exceptional, if not downright mind-boggling rates, to make just a modest return on something which is costing you 10 to 13 percent per annum. It rarely happens. Usually, interest costs exceed the appreciation and THE DEBT LEVER WORKS IN REVERSE.

I recall a classic example of this reality. Reece shared with me (without mentioning specifics) a statement made by a gentleman who came into his office one day to list a farm for sale. It epitomizes the whole syndrome. The man said, "It was the best doggone investment I ever made; if I could have just hung on another year. But the interest just keeps wringing me."

OTHER DEBT TRAPS

Leveraged real estate is not the only debt trap, of course. In reality, it would exceed the capacity of this book to attempt to catalogue and explain the myriad ways one can shoot oneself in the foot with debt.

I cannot move on, however, without mentioning at least one more trap. This debt snare was also a major component of my physician friend's downfall. I refer to the "Appearance Of Wealth Begets Wealth" game. There is a questionable dictum in the business world that is held to be one of the basic veracities of commerce. You cannot start or expand a business without biting off a hunk of debt. Translated another way, it is the belief that in order to get to be a big business, you must appear to be a big business or people won't buy your stuff.

I am not saying that image and positioning are not business realities. They are; and they are *very* important. I am not recommending that you neglect these critical elements of marketing. However, I am saying that, too often, people will go off the deep end with that in business and personal life. Never expand your lifestyle as a ploy to promote your business. Projecting the "successful image" can backfire, if taken too far. You do not need a huge mansion or a ruby-encrusted board room to verify that your business is sound.

A perfectly superb example of this lies very close to home. I have a younger brother. I am very fond of him, but he did something almost unspeakable for a younger brother to do — *he* became a millionaire before I did. Other than that atrocity, he is not only a brother, but a friend. My precocious sibling became a millionaire in just over five years, by founding a business and nursing it through all the growth and expansion times without going into copious amounts of debt as the false map makers would contend.

Today, as throughout his ascent to wealth, he expands on his own money. He will not borrow. He now has a great little company, doing business all over the world, employing four to five dozen people and making obscene amounts of money. He has kept it simple, and he and his partner have kept themselves free and clear of the debilitating shackles of "business expansion and investment debt."

There were times when he was sorely tempted to borrow and "play the part." He started his dream fairly unprepared. In August of 1983, he quit a perfectly good job with AT&T to, along with a partner, go for his dream. They did not even have an office the day he walked up to his boss and resigned. In retrospect he said, "Working for AT&T for all those years, you would think we'd have known it takes at least two weeks to even get a phone."

They started by renting a dumpy little warehouse and putting in a couple of tables for desks. It was far from posh, it was almost an embarrassment, but they fought the temptation to capitalize with borrowed dollars and lease a fancier setting. They made do.

When the need arose for more attractive surroundings, they had to get a little creative. One time a prospective client—a manufacturer's representative with no small clout—wanted to pay a visit on them. He wanted to meet them face to face, and get better acquainted. That is the one moment they felt they really did *need* some reasonably presentable quarters.

Ingenuity prevailed. They had a friend who was going out of the town and was willing to rent out his office, complete with secretary, computers and paper clips. My brother and his partner spent a few dollars on signs and marquee labels and, almost like you see in the movies, made the transition in a few hours' time. They greeted their representative at the airport, took him to their "office," held their meeting, took the man back to the airport, went back and replaced the signs on their friend's door and marquee, and slipped quietly back into their humble little warehouse in the slums.

Using their heads instead of their credit, the effort stood them in good stead, and not only saved money, the discipline paved the way for their eventual success.

Making every nickel count, they forged ahead. They struggled, and there were times when it did not look like they would make it. More than once, they had to employ courage and creativity to build their business while making ends meet at home. But they kept it "lean and mean" at home *and* in the business, and eventually they made it. And when they did, they did not have to flush a lot of the profits away in interest or share their cache with anyone else.

He and his partner could retire today. Neither is yet 40. Their business is growing like mad, they are putting a hunk of money in the bank every month, they have their homes paid for... and the road was not paved with debt.

There is a second part to the story. Fairly early on, my brother and his partner hired an employee who thought they were idiots. She thought there was a better way. They were far too conservative in her estimation. They were not fancy enough. They needed to have expensive, glossy brochures, an office with image, located in the most prestigious high-rise.

Finally, her suggestions unheeded, she left and decided to go into competition with them and show them how it should be done. She borrowed a huge sum of money from an affluent relative, rented a plush office with all the appointments and trappings, and put up the kind of "image that really makes a statement." She didn't last a year.

My brother and his partner kept it modest and debt-free. Now, they have all the appointments and amenities, too. But it is not an image. It is the *real* substance of *real* success. It is so much smarter to *be* rich than merely seem rich. That is the ultimate deceit of borrowed dollars. When you have earned them, you know what they are worth. The hard work sharpens your mind and your perspective stays clear. You spend only when the value is really there. The thrift and restraint breed better decision-making. It is much easier to be frivolous with borrowed dollars than earned dollars. Herein is the difference: Discipline brings strength; the strength brings success. Borrowing does not beget such a formula.

BE WISE. GET STRONG. REMEMBER, THE ROAD TO FINANCIAL FREEDOM IS NOT PAVED WITH DEBT.

CHAPTER 7

Write-off Heaven

Another favorite harangue of the false map makers pronounces that only fools pay taxes. They say taxes must be avoided *at all costs*. Even worse, this fallacy leads all too many people to pounce to yet another conclusion which markedly compounds the original fallacy. Without thinking, they manage to proceed to the deduction that anything that reduces taxes creates wealth. I am sorry, but that is *not* an automatic equation. There is no direct cause and effect relationship between the not paying of taxes and getting rich.

FALLACY NO. 5:

ONLY FOOLS PAY TAXES.

This fallacy is so enticing because Americans have an almost inbred loathing for taxes anyway. The issue of taxation was the thorn in the colonists' side which led ultimately to the Declaration of Independence. We decided to fight the greatest military power on the face of the earth at that time, Imperial England, rather than pay the taxes. Still today, we love to quote Benjamin Franklin and his sardonic quip, "In this world nothing is certain but death and taxes," and then we faithfully add something like, "Yes, but death doesn't get worse every time Congress meets."

As the government steadily increases its fondling of our wallets and purses, we long for the good old days (1817-1862) when there were no domestic taxes of any kind. One of the legacies of the Civil War was the establishment of the Commissioner of Internal Revenue, a position which somehow hung around after the need to fund the war had vanished.

As we approach one of the trickiest junctions on our journey, I need to make something plain. I am proud to be a United States' citizen. I love this country, but I am not advocating paying any more taxes than legally necessary. I firmly agree with Wall Street's F.J. Raymond: "Next to being shot at and missed, nothing is quite as satisfying as an income tax refund." We definitely want to keep our tax payments to a minimum.

The peril befalling many people at the intersection with Highway 1040 is that they, for some reason, totally lose their bearings and head off toward a deceitfully specious destination. The turn on the false map reads, "AVOID TAXES AT ALL COSTS."

Quoting from a best-selling financial advice book:

> If you are planning on becoming wealthy you should have an inherent dislike for all destroyers of wealth. The paying of taxes is one of the greatest wealth destroyers of all.

Be careful. The biggest destroyer of wealth is stupidity. The paying of some modest taxes is often less stupid than the ploys to avoid paying any taxes at all. Once again, recall my physician friend (you met him in Chapter 2). One of the binds he got into, a bind which lures and traps unwary travelers every day, is the "Great Write-off Bind." Sometimes (as a physician should have known) the cure is worse than the disease.

There are books written and seminars taught on the subject of tax avoidance, and some of the information is solid and worth applying. However, too often, people get carried away with the fever of it all (unbridled passion again) and lose sight of the objective, which is to *accumulate* wealth. I caution you to keep the *real* objective clearly in mind. Avoiding taxes is not the objective. The goal is to amass a pile of money. Seems obvious, I know, but it is amazing how often people get so obsessed with tax avoidance their compass goes haywire. When that happens, they end up decimating their wallets and destroying their peace of mind.

What makes Fallacy No. 5 especially insidious is that it neatly links up with Fallacy No. 4 and makes debt and leverage appear to be clever tax reduction strategies. Debt and leverage *do* reduce taxes. That is because they devastate income. You pay less taxes, alright, but you have not accumulated money, you have accumulated receipts. Especially around the month of April do we become attracted to this trap. It has been said, if you want to sell something to the masses one of two ploys will work: Tell them it is on sale, or tell them it is tax deductible.

Some of the things I teach in this book have more than just monetary or financial applications. Take the above for instance. For some inexplicable reason, men seem exceptionally vulnerable to the tax deduction ploy. To the women, I have now disclosed a formidable weapon. Not even the Sirens of Greece could do better. If you want to keep the fire and romance in your relationship, you need not spend money on lacy negligees or expensive perfumes. All you must do to get your man's motor humming is slip up behind him, embrace him gently, and in a low, provocative tone, whisper, "Write-off, write-off, write-off." *Nothing* seems to get a man breathing heavy like the word, *"Write-off."* (I recently shared this valuable piece of wisdom with a short, perky lady sitting next to me on an airplane. She seemed absolutely *elated* with this little pearl. Said her name was Ruth something.)

I am being only partially facetious here. In reality, it is surprising how many reasonably sane people completely lose their bearings over this issue of deductions. Again, the objective is to accumulate money, not write-offs. You are trying to keep money, not play paper games of how benignly you can lose it.

Take all the deductions you can. Write off an unfortunate loss when it occurs. *But*, do not lose sight of the fact that a deduction on the 1040 Form is not an addition to your estate. It is a minus there, also. To this day, it still boggles my mind how many people fail to recognize that fact. The IRS only lets you deduct a paltry percentage of losses and write-offs from your tax bill. However, as opposed to that small percentage you claimed on Form 1040, *every* penny of a loss is subtracted from your net worth. Yet, some people will almost rejoice in a write-off or a loss, as though any reduction in taxes somehow makes them rich.

Too many people allow the IRS regulations and the fear of paying some taxes to become the governing forces in their financial decisions. "What will save me the most taxes?" is the most frequently asked question in investment decisions. Those whose investment and monetary decisions are wholly "tax form driven" are steering with blinders on and one eye closed.

The questions that should be asked are more along these lines: "Does the venture make sense and have a high probability of success totally on its own merit? Tax benefits aside, does it make money?" And, the real acid test: "Would I enter this venture if it actually had some mild tax *dis*advantages?" (Like, if it would actually make you a substantial *profit*.) Believe me, I have done intensive personal research on the subject, and my findings clearly indicate that it is impossible to get wealthy by losing money; but, you *will* save taxes if *that* is your goal.

Use a little common sense. Do not turn the cure into a disease all its own. Don't get too aggressive or innovative, fabricating deductions and write-offs. Will Rogers, one of this century's most astute political critics, observed:

> The income tax has made more liars out of the American people than golf has. Even when you make a tax form out on the level, you don't know, when it's through, if you are a crook or a martyr.

When you stretch the limits of the tax law or "creatively embellish," you pay a price in worry and distraction. If you get too cute, too aggressive, or too flamboyant, the specter of a nasty tax audit lurks doggedly over your shoulder, haunting you from time to time. Draw the line and stay on the side of reason. You will sleep better. Your mind will be free to focus on things which matter a great deal more than taxes.

Avoid losses, deduct what you can, pay some tax, and go on with the weightier matters of life. There is a lot more to life than NOT PAYING TAXES. Avoiding taxes at all costs, *costs*!

A CASE OF WRITE-OFF BLINDNESS

A few years ago I met an orthodontist who was constantly bragging about paying no income tax. It seemed like he would *try* to bring it into the conversation. He would mention it at parties, on the golf course—whenever he wanted to impress someone. I kept getting the feeling that he had lost sight of the real objective in all this.

One day the opportunity presented itself; "I understand you have not paid much income tax the past few years," I said.

"Not a penny for the last four years now," he responded.

"How much did you pay in interest last year?" I asked.

"Counting everything," (we are talking home, office, office equipment and furnishings, boat, cabin, credit cards, three automobiles, student loans and who knows what else) he said, "over $100,000. But I wrote it all off."

And there, is the truth in simple English—"HE WROTE IT *ALL* OFF." That is the entire point: He wrote it all off—every penny—all $100,000, right off his books. It all went through his checkbook, out the door, and down the street. However, he did *not* write *ALL* of it off his taxes. He was only allowed to deduct a percentage of that amount off his taxable income. (Ain't Uncle Sam generous?)

To further illustrate, suppose my friend, the orthodontist, had no write-offs and had not paid even one cent in interest. He would have had to declare all $100,000 as taxable income. Since this incident occurred before the 1986 tax law changes, that would have put him in a 50 percent tax bracket. (Today, the maximum bracket is 31 percent.)

Given all of the above, this is what he would have been looking at on April 15th: Our friend, the orthodontist, would have had to pay the IRS $50,000—a flat half of that nice $100,000. Without question, it would have stung the day he wrote out the check. Yet, there is something else to consider.

If he had not shoveled all that money down the road to his creditors and had retained it, yes, he would have had to pay $50,000 to Uncle Sam, but do you know what he would have had to do with the other half—the other $50,000? HE WOULD HAVE BEEN FORCED TO *KEEP* IT! Now can you see the beauty of his strategy? (In the dictionary, when you look up the word "shrewd," I'll bet his picture is next to it.)

Just keep one thing in mind: A WRITE-OFF IS MERELY A METHOD OF DETERMINING WHERE THE MONEY YOU DON'T GET GOES.

Don't tell me only fools pay taxes. There are a lot of poor fools out there who pay little or no taxes; the maneuvers, calisthenics, and contortions they go through to save a dollar on taxes are often more devastating to their financial goals, and to their lives, than the paying of the taxes would be.

THE P.I.T.S. TOLL ROAD

Another neat little toll road to nowhere is the Perfectly Ingenious Tax Shelter (PITS) Boulevard. This charming little thoroughfare purports to take you on a pleasant and scenic route to a lush retirement location, but, in reality, it comes to an abrupt dead end. With only part of the dollars that have been lost on PITS

Boulevard, we could turn the tables on the Japanese and go buy *their* land.

With more and more of us making more and more dollars, more and more of us are becoming acquainted with its environs, especially since most of us have heard and have come to believe implicitly, "Only fools pay taxes."

For those of you who have not driven down this shady and inviting street, let me briefly explain the general parameters of what constitutes the PITS. Usually we have some ostensibly reputable people with "immense business acumen" and a long history of "very successful enterprises" who come to us and say, "Would you like to save money on your tax bill?" Great line. Who wouldn't?—"Only fools pay taxes." Remember that they use the word, "*SAVE*". We will return to that later on for further clarification. Just remember for now that they employ the crucial word, "save."

Usually this respectable consortium presents itself on the doorstep in November or December with a stridently urgent reminder that we need to act before the year ends or we will not benefit from the tax savings on the present year's burden. (That colorful pennant you see waving on our left, by the way, is a red flag.) "Check things out carefully," they admonish, "but do not dally. You must act before it is too late." (Now the sidewalk is alive with crimson flags.) Enjoying the forecasted good weather, we fail to see anything but bliss on the boulevard, and we proceed.

Then these gentle people explain how they can *save* us bundles on our taxes. They have a PITS which we can take advantage of. In order to do so, we must take a fair hunk of cash— the more we "invest" (another key word), the more taxes we will save—and put it into their carefully planned and prudently managed PITS. They explain that once the money is deposited with them it is very illiquid. They must make it so in order to keep on the up and up as a legitimate tax shelter in the eyes of the IRS. During the time our money is tied up, however, (we are assured) all of the managers in the PITS will be working their trustworthy little fingers to the bone, laboring around the clock, making sure that our investment (there's that word again) is growing and growing and growing.

Eventually, they are pleased to explain, all of our money will come back to us along with an excitingly handsome increase. They are positive they can at least double or treble our original lump, and they allude to multiples much higher than that. During this growth period, they add, beaming all the while, we will not have to pay one cent of taxes. Although we will *eventually* have to pay some taxes, they admit, our gargantuan gains will more than compensate. This grand cash-in day will take place some 20 to 25 years down the road. By then, they point out, we will be retired and bringing in less income, putting us in a much lower tax bracket, and thus ("ALAKAZAM") we will have saved a fortune in taxes.

We are assured that it is all perfectly safe, perfectly ingenious, and perfectly perfect. That, ladies and gentlemen, is the pitch line which gets people to queue up to get into the PITS. Once on the way, however, the road leads to destinations not included in the jaunty little prospectus or in the glib explanations by our sincere salesperson. Actually, there are times when we even get the feeling that part of the boulevard is still under construction even as we travel.

For instance, somewhere along the line, the IRS sends us not a happy note. We are informed that they have looked into the PITS and are not all that impressed with it. They declare that it is nothing more than a way to circumvent taxes and they would be very pleased to collect their share of the money we put confidingly into the PITS. We are taken back by the tone they use: They accuse us of deliberate deceit and inform us that we could stand to experience severe legal floggings unless we choose to cough up the money that should have been paid some time ago, together with interest and penalty; and all of this, of course, is due...NOW!

Assuring the IRS that our intentions were not nearly so criminal as they have construed, we quickly backpedal over to our friends at the PITS (who have been working around the clock, expanding our money to gargantuan sums). When we arrive, the secretary informs us that all of the managers are out of the office, (out there working all those fingers to the bone, no doubt) and that we should read the fine print in our contract. This reaffirms how illiquid the PITS is and, although they are sorry the IRS viewed it otherwise, we cannot get the money necessary to pay the tax bill out of their program.

So, we scrape up *more* money, enough to pay the taxes (and penalty and interest) on the money which we earned but never really benefited from. We did not even take the opportunity to blow it on frivolous expenditures (like food, clothing, or shelter). Nonetheless, we take solace in the fact that there is still going to be that gargantuan sum to retire on *and* we will have just that much less tax to pay at retirement. We are still motoring down PITS Boulevard, faith intact.

Not long after that, we receive a crisp letter from the hard-working people over at the PITS. They regretfully inform us that some of their original projections will need to be modified downward, and, while all is still well and our principal is still safely intact, things are not going as well as had been originally anticipated. Every attempt is being made to make up for some delays, and *semi*-gargantuan sums are still anticipated.

Two weeks later (or less) as we are skimming through the evening newspaper, near the obituary section, we read a short article detailing the bankruptcy of the PITS. And the day after that comes a letter from the PITS saying, (skipping all of the financial and legal mumbo jumbo) "CIAO!"

PITS Boulevard ends abruptly. No tax savings. No cushy retirement. Dead end. This turns out to be a *very* expensive toll road. And the only gargantuan thing we come away with is disappointment, embarrassment and regret.

A vice president for a well-known brokerage house (who prefers to remain anonymous for job security reasons), is quoted as saying:

> I'll sell a tax shelter when I hear of one that pays its investors their money back, let alone profit. So far, I've never heard of a single one.

Write this down! THE RETURN *OF* YOUR PRINCIPAL IS MORE IMPORTANT THAN THE RETURN *ON* YOUR PRINCIPAL. If you lose your principal you haven't sheltered a thing.

STRATEGY CHECK

Before you ever begin to weigh the merits or minuses of *any* tax shelter, carefully examine the entire strategy to see if you even want it in the first place. I question the value of the whole premise. And I certainly do not think the risk-to-benefit ratio has any appeal whatsoever.

Let one thing become very clear in your mind. There is no such thing as tax SAVINGS. At best it is only tax POSTPONE-MENT. Sooner or later Uncle Sam is going to get his share. Count on it.

The edge the folks in the PITS are really hawking is only an assumption, anyway. History testifies that it is a flimsy assumption. The rationale is, at retirement, you will *probably* be earning less and, therefore, you will *probably* be in a lower tax bracket. Therefore, you will *probably* pay a lower percentage of tax, and so Uncle Sam's share will (you guessed it) *probably* be less. The reason for all the uncertainty is that Uncle Sam has the right to change the rules of the game any time Congress, in its infinite wisdom, wishes to.

If you take an historical perspective of this matter, you begin to detect a conspicuous trend. As time marches on, Uncle

Sam's share tends to go up. A rule of thumb starts to dawn in one's mind. The more time you give him, the more he succeeds in taking.

One begins to get an eerie feeling about the whole idea of tax *postponement*. The truth is, trends are not in the taxpayer's favor. In the past, the longer you stalled, the greater the tax bite tended to be. The future looks even more ominous. Tax postponement *today*, with a burgeoning national debt looming at our door, may prove, in the approaching decades, to be a very disappointing strategy. Sooner or later, the books are going to be balanced; and guess who will foot the bill? The *future* taxpayers of America.

I'm still in favor of self-directed IRAs and well-managed tax deferred retirement plans. We'll touch more upon them in the Master Plan. Do not become overly obsessed deferring income and taxes. Again, we come to a common sense conclusion: Take all the precautions and lawful deductions you can, but keep it reasonable, keep it simple. Pay some taxes, and keep your sanity, your dignity and your peace of mind. (And, good night Mrs. Helmsley, wherever you are.)

CHAPTER 8

Changing Times

It is incredible how effectively the words "NEW AND IMPROVED" work on the minds of human beings. The phrase is actually self-contradictory; but, time and time again, it works. Although this is usually the eye-catching *opener* on all the false maps, I have saved this one for last. Virtually every book on the "One-minute Millionaire" shelf starts with verbiage to the effect that TIMES ARE DIFFERENT NOW.

FALLACY NO 6:

TIMES ARE DIFFERENT NOW.

The only thing that differs is the degree of alarm the authors choose to infuse into their pitch. Some are moderately subdued, while others attempt to work the reader into a fevered hysteria. Some would have you believe that the world is already (even as you read) in the latter stages of an economic apocalypse which will destroy governments and all socio-economic order. In such scenarios, you barely have enough time to save yourself and your estate. You will have to act fast.

After administering whatever doses of alarm seem appropriate, the authors "modestly" offer their book as the ultimate solution. Theirs is a *new* approach; and, of course, only they can supply the one and only answer to economic salvation. What else can they say? They are not going to sell many books if they confide that their method is merely a speculation, while the reader could follow the proven methods (which were even old in Ben Franklin's day and, by golly, they will still work today).

The level of sophistication may vary, but the essence of their "theology" is this: Never before in the entire history of civilization have we encountered the unprecedented melange of economic fragments confronting mankind at this juncture in time. This admixture of stunningly unique perplexities makes all previous strategies woefully obsolete. The sound principles and practices of the past, which have worked well decade upon decade, will no longer succeed. They must be summarily rejected; and in their stead must come the revolutionarily *new* and astutely *improved* techniques of the sage author. That come-on is the leading line in the oldest cons in the world. Whenever you hear such doctrine, my advice to you is CAVEAT EMPTOR (Buyer Beware). More explicitly, RUN!

I have always had a hard time believing that, in any endeavor, correct principles come and go. That is the central difference between a principle and a technique. If something is truly a principle, it is substantially unaffected by superficial and transient conditions. Techniques, on the other hand, are highly circumstantial.

Simply put: Principles take precedence over techniques.

The economic conditions which exist today are not without precedent. Facades change, but the essences do not. Adopting an economic game plan which will be effective in any climate is possible; and it is based on well-proven principles that will not fail. They are not glamorous. They just work.

TIME TO GROW UP

Part of growing up is the putting away of cherished childhood fantasies—The Tooth Fairy, The Easter Bunny, and Lady Luck. To become a healthy, fully mature person, one must learn to take complete responsibility for oneself, and stop self-deceptive mental practices. Prospector's Mentality is one such deception.

Success, high achievement, and wealth, in the full and genuine sense, are attained by compliance with the principles and laws which yield them. In the universe, every effect has a cause. Nothing happens capriciously. There is no such thing as luck. There is, instead, a just and inviolable Law of the Harvest. As you sow, so shall you reap. That is a basic tenet of life.

No amount of rationalization or self-deception will ever change those immutable laws of the universe. Rationalization only delays or precludes the harvest. The longer one dallies, the longer the postponement. Dally long enough, and there will be no harvest at all. Sooner or later it all boils down to a single truth: Financial freedom is based and built on self-mastery and self-mastery only.

A major milestone in human growth and maturity is achieved when one ceases the courtship of Lady Luck and rejects, once and for all, Prospector's Mentality. To claim belief in the law of the harvest, yet to keep seeking for a quick, easy route to luxury, is self-duplicity of the first order.

IF YOU REALLY BELIEVE IN THE LAW OF THE HARVEST, THEN STOP PROSPECTING AND START *FARMING*!!

SECTION II

THE PARAMETERS

You will not find until you know where to seek.

The major defect in the Acquirement Maps is that they have no end. They do not reach a culmination. People who follow them never arrive; they only pursue. Conversely, the major advantage of the Accumulation Map is that it is not only measurable, but you can bring it to a defined culmination. Section II will help you gain the needed insights to fill in the detail and specificity for a correct and successful Accumulation Map.

CHAPTER 9

The Wisdom of the Ages: Still In Style

Most of the people who will read this book will be doing so because they presently find themselves in severe financial straits. They have already taken some wrong turns and have fallen victim to one or more of the ploys heralded by the false map makers.

Those who have lived correct principles unerringly from their youth are already in the fast lane on the freeway to financial freedom. They do not need this book except as a pat on the back and source of positive reinforcement as they teach these concepts to their offspring.

Therefore, I want to assure all of you, who are mired in some financial quagmires and who may be broken down and stranded on some remote and desolate detour, that this book is expressly written with you in mind. Regardless of your present situation you *can* get back on the Road to Accumulation and you can still achieve a rewarding destination.

If it brings any comfort and encouragement to you, I am not adverse to plainly confessing that my perspectives and the insights which have led to the writing of this book have been obtained and refined by the things which I have suffered. I have received vivid instruction in the school of personal experience.

To you, the lone and weary traveller, I pass on the essence of my expensive education, hoping it will provide you with ample encouragement, useful and workable ideas, and will spare you grief.

BEN'S MAP

The principles for a correct map have been around for a long time. There is no end to the irony of that. The territory has been mapped out for centuries. It pre-dates the founding of the United States. It was ancient wisdom in Benjamin Franklin's day. Hear his own admission from his classic treatise, *The Way to Wealth*, which was published in 1758:

> Not a tenth part of the wisdom he ascribed to me was my own, but rather the gleanings I had made of the sense of all ages and nations.

Franklin's wisdom was not complex; and it still works today.

He taught these principles:

1. Work Hard

2. Live Providently

3. Avoid Debt

4. Harness Compounding

Here are some samples of what Franklin had to say:

1. WORK HARD

"The taxes are indeed very heavy, and if those laid on by the government were the only ones we had to pay, we might more easily discharge them; but we have many others, and much more grievous to some of us. We are taxed twice as much by our idleness..."

"God helps them that help themselves."

"Sloth, like rust, consumes faster than labor wears. The used key is always bright."

"The sleeping fox catches no poultry."

"Sloth makes all things difficult, but industry all easy. Laziness travels so slowly that poverty soon overtakes him."

"Then plough deep while sluggards sleep, and you shall have corn to sell and keep."

2. LIVE PROVIDENTLY

"A man may, if he knows not how to save as he gets, keep his nose all his life to the grindstone, and die not worth a groat at last." (He spends too much money on nose reconstructive surgery, I posit.)

"Tis easier to suppress the first desire than to satisfy all that follow it."

"Pride breakfasted with plenty, dined with poverty, and supped with infamy."

"Beware of little expenses; a small leak will sink a great ship."

"At a great pennyworth pause a while, many have been ruined by buying good pennyworths."

3. AVOID DEBT

"He that goes a borrowing goes a sorrowing."

"But what madness must it be to run in debt for these superfluities (Fancy clothing, dainty cakes, etc)....But, ah, think what you do when you run in debt; you give to another power over your liberty!"

"Those have a short Lent, who owe money to be paid at Easter."

"Rather go to bed supperless than rise in debt."

4. HARNESS COMPOUNDING

Franklin not only taught the power of thrift, he lived the principle of compounding. As an example, he bestowed on the cities of Boston and Philadelphia an endowment of 1000 pounds each. The endowments were to be untouched for 100 years. Through the miracle of compounding, a large sum would result which would benefit the cities in perpetuity.

Nearly 200 years after the initial gift, Boston and Philadelphia still enjoy the benefits of Franklin's industry, thrift, and wise use of interest. Everything from city development (and redevelopment) to scholarships for medical students have been financed by this wisdom.

THE RICHEST MAN IN BABYLON

In 1926 George Samuel Clason began publishing a series of "Babylonian Parables" dealing with personal financial management. They were later published together in book form under the title of the best known of these short allegories. That book, *The Richest Man In Babylon*, has since become a classic with over 2 million copies in print. There is little question in my mind that Clason's book has helped more people achieve financial peace of mind than any other book on earth. I strongly endorse its concepts and recommend that you get a copy and read it at least once a year for the rest of your life.

The richest man in Babylon is a man named Arkad who learned a grand secret in his youth. By a wealthy elder, he is taught that A PART OF ALL HE EARNS IS HIS TO KEEP.

At first Arkad does not comprehend the grand import of that nugget, and claims in rebuttal that *all* he earns is his to keep. Forcefully his wise mentor jolts Arkad into reality by pointing out that if all his monthly earnings pass through his fingers as he pays his living expenses, he is little more than a slave, working for his food and raiment. Unless Arkad pays himself first, keeping part of his income so it may work for him, he will never find his way out of the bondage of monthly labor.

Once the discipline of saving a part of each month's wages is mastered, Arkad learns other important truths from his teacher, including the power of compound interest.

It has been my experience that the individuals who are truly free financially and who experience monetary peace of mind, apply the THREE CENTRAL PRINCIPLES contained in that simple story. They will work for you too. You must:

1. Live on less than you earn.

2. Pay yourself first.

3. Let your savings compound.

LIVE ON LESS THAN YOU EARN

The key to spending less than one earns is DISCIPLINE. Unless and until you learn monetary self-discipline, a little more money will not solve your problems since it is not possible to earn more than you are able to spend. Emerson said, "Money can be an obedient servant, but a harsh taskmaster."

Sooner or later each of us must learn to distinguish between needs and wants. Our desires are insatiable unless bridled by fixed purpose and self-control. Most of the things we suffer in life are consequences of throwing away what we want most for what we want *now*.

Nothing will bring more order, serenity and wealth to your life than living *within* your income. Income alone is not sufficient. Living within that income is the key. "The Indies have not made Spain rich, because her outgoes are greater than her incomes," was another of Franklin's astute observations in *The Way To Wealth*. Those individuals who structure their lifestyle to allow a modest surplus, CONTROL THEIR DESTINY BECAUSE THEY CONTROL THEMSELVES, AND THEY ENJOY PEACE OF MIND.

This principle is fundamental and it is essential. If you do not learn this one lesson, nothing else I or anyone else has to say will matter. This is the foundation of wealth, and the beginning of financial freedom.

PAY YOURSELF FIRST

Put yourself on salary; you are worth it. Pay yourself at least 10 percent of your income no matter how little or how much you make.

The first check you should disburse each month should be to your savings account. Do not think that you can keep it in your checking account. Put it into a passbook or money market account until you have enough to roll into a CD (Certificate of Deposit). Learn to live on the remaining 90 percent.

I am sure you have heard the statement, "It's like money in the bank." Pause for a moment, and think about that phrase. "It's like money in the bank," is a superlative—a synonym for the ultimate in "having it made." Why? Because money in the bank is insured, it's real, and its earnings are real. There are no paper profits that are difficult to convert. No ambiguity. No fantasy. Not many things bring greater calm or serenity than having a cozy little nest egg in a liquid form in a solid institution, growing at a gradual, yet unrelenting, rate.

THIS IS NOT AN INVESTMENT. BUT, IT IS THE FOUNDATION FROM WHICH YOU WILL LAUNCH SUC-CESSFUL INVESTMENTS.

LET YOUR SAVINGS COMPOUND

Let the POWER OF COMPOUNDING WORK FOR YOU!!

Venita Van Caspel, a well-known author and financial consultant, lives in Houston, Texas. She flatly states, "In my opinion, the 'eighth wonder of the world' is not the Astrodome, but compound interest!"

To appreciate Ms. Van Caspel's high esteem for compounding, you need to clearly see the difference between simple interest and compound interest:

Simple Interest - Interest paid only on the principal. Any interest accrued is viewed to accumulate apart from the principal and no interest is paid on accumulated interest.

Compound Interest - Interest paid on principal *and* the accrued interest. At designated intervals (monthly, quarterly, annually) accrued interest is added to the principal and interest accrues on that *sum* until the next interval. At each interval, the total amount gaining interest increases. The interest of each interval is added, which also gains interest, thus markedly enhancing the effective yield.

SIMPLE INTEREST VS. COMPOUND INTEREST

On the next page is an economic table which will illustrate the advantageous power of compounding. The initial amount is the same. In each case a lump sum of $10,000 is deposited. Both accounts receive 8 percent per annum.

However, one account earns simple interest, while the other has the interest compounded quarterly.

	SIMPLE INTEREST			**COMPOUND INTEREST**		
Yr.	Principal	Interest	Total	Principal	Interest	Total
1	$10,000	$200	$10,200	$10,000	$200	$10,200
	10,000	200	10,400	10,200	204	10,404
	10,000	200	10,600	10,404	208	10,612
	10,000	200	10,800	10,612	212	10,824
2	10,000	200	11,000	10,812	216	11,041
	10,000	200	11,200	11,041	221	11,262
	10,000	200	11,400	11,262	225	11,487
	10,000	200	11,600	11,487	230	11,717
3	10,000	200	11,800	11,717	234	11,951
	10,000	200	12,000	11,951	239	12,190
	10,000	200	12,200	12,190	244	12,434
	10,000	200	12,400	12,434	249	12,682
4	10,000	200	12,600	12,682	254	12,936
	10,000	200	12,800	12,936	259	13,195
	10,000	200	13,000	13,195	264	13,459
	10,000	200	13,200	13,459	269	13,728

As time passes, the difference becomes distinct and, eventually, quite noteworthy. After the subsequent six years the table looks like this:

	SIMPLE INTEREST			**COMPOUND INTEREST**		
Yr.	Principal	Interest	Total	Principal	Interest	Total
5	$10,000	$200	$14,000	$14,568	$291	$14,859
6	10,000	200	14,800	15,769	315	16,084
7	10,000	200	15,600	17,069	341	17,410
8	10,000	200	16,400	18,476	370	18,845
9	10,000	200	17,200	19,999	400	20,399
10	10,000	200	18,000	21,647	433	22,080

Over the 10-year period, the annual rate is the same in both cases. However, compounding results in a net gain of $4,080.

PETER MINUIT AND THE INDIANS

Many of us have heard in a long-ago U.S. history class that a Peter Minuit, of the Dutch West India Company made a fortuitous land purchase from a naive tribe of native Americans. Minuit is supposed to have "purchased" the entire island of Manhattan for $24 worth of costume jewelry.

"Skillful shopping," the history teacher said. This seemingly appropriate quip was made in light of the fact that the land Minuit obtained is now the primest of prime "beach front property." Even by conservative appraisals, the value of this tidy little parcel of real estate is in excess of $20 billion.

This land investment has grown impressively, but another rationale is also rather instructive. Observe what would have happened to the Minuit family fortune, if Peter had banked that $24 and received a 6 percent return (compounded annually):

YEAR	DOLLAR VALUE
1626	$24
1726	$8,143
1826	$2,763,022
1926	$937,499,017
1992	$78,562,732,677

Rather than a $20 billion parcel of land, which they would have had to maintain and manage, the Minuits could have had a $78 billion bank account. By the 400th anniversary of the "great land deal," the year 2026, the Minuit bank account would stand at over $318 billion. Even if the Japanese were to get into a bidding war among themselves and go merrily buying up Manhattan, it is inconceivable that the real estate venture would outpay the compound interest route.

Here is another example of the power of compounding:

LUMP SUM OF $25,000 AT 8 PERCENT

Suppose that you inherited a lump sum of $25,000 at age 30, and that you could average an annual interest rate of 8 percent, compounded annually. Here is how your lump would grow:

5 years	$36,733
10 years	$53,973
15 years	$79,304
20 years	$116,524
25 years	$171,212
30 years	$251,566
35 years	$369,634

If you will remember the introspective quiz I extended in Chapter 1, you will see the point. Hanging onto the money—not letting it slip away the moment you get it—brings substantial rewards down the road.

I have had people sneer at this. They claim they can do much better than 8 percent per year. (But they always seem to squirm a little when I pop a one-word question at them, "Consistently?") An unfailing 8 percent per year is nothing to sneeze at, but my pleasant surprise for you is that, through the miracle of compounding, you have actually done better than that.

What percentage growth did you actually get on your $25,000? Subtracting the original sum, you have gained roughly $344,000 over and above your initial $25,000. That is an increase of 1,376 percent! If you divide that by 35 years, you find that you have made *excellent* growth on your money. You have actually averaged 39.3 percent growth *each year*!

That is the miracle of compounding. Each year's gain is added to the principal so you are gaining on the gain. The effect is truly amazing and very rewarding when *you* are the lender. And, frankly, I don't see too many investments out there that will yield that kind of return, year in and year out. Plus, if you pick the right vehicle (more on that later) you have low risk and no maintenance worries.

THE INFLATION FACTOR

It is precisely at this juncture that the prospectors want to raise an objection. They dredge up the big, bad inflation factor, protesting that this strategy is too naive because it does not keep pace with inflation. Saving is dumb, they contend, because inflation is going to reduce the buying power of your dollar down the road.

First, may I reiterate that no one is denying the existence of inflation here. The dollar is going to decline in purchasing power with the passage of time. It is going to do that whether I speculate or whether I save. (My personal monetary policies seem to have negligible effect on the world. You may take comfort in that, I suppose.) Notwithstanding all that, the miracle of compounding still has merit.

If you take the actual historical reality of the effect of inflation on the purchasing power of the dollar from 1952 to 1987 (35 years), the documented fact is that the dollar lost approximately 78 percent of its value.

In other words it took four and one-half dollars in 1987 to buy what you could buy in 1952 with one dollar.

So, let's put the inflation factor into our example and see if there was a gain or loss in actual purchasing power. If we take $369,634 and divide it by 4 1/2, we will have put 1987 dollars into the 1952 context.

$$\frac{\$369,634}{4.5} = \$82,141$$

In other words, $82,141 in 1952 would buy what $369,634 would buy in 1987. (If this shocks you a bit, relax—I will give you better news later on.) So, in terms of the original frame of reference (1952) we *have* made a gain. Our $25,000 has grown to $82,141 in equivalent purchasing power.

Despite the ravages of inflation, we have still forged ahead. It may not be as dramatic as you first thought, but you are still ahead of the game. The fact is you have more than trebled your purchasing power. (And without excessive risk or the distraction and hassles associated with prospecting and speculation.)

It must be pointed out that the real power in compounding comes in the *latter* stages. The sooner you get to harnessing this power, the more dramatic its effects in your behalf.

Let me illustrate the point with the following table:

$25,000 AT 8 PERCENT, COMPOUNDED ANNUALLY

Time	Total Amt.	Gain	% Gain	% Gain Per Year
5 years	$36,733	$11,733	47	9.4
10 years	$53,973	$28,973	116	11.6
15 years	$79,304	$54,304	217	14.5
20 years	$116,524	$91,524	366	18.3
25 years	$171,212	$146,212	585	23.4
30 years	$251,566	$226,566	906	30.2
35 years	$369,634	$344,634	1379	39.4

This table dramatically illustrates that the greatest benefits from compounding are accrued in the *long-term* context. Each year you let the money grow, in effect, increases the value of each of the preceding years. If you leave the money at work for 20 years, you have actually gained 18.3 percent on your money *each year*. But, if the money is at work for an additional 5 years, the percent gained *for each year* increases to 23.4 percent.

There are at least two lessons to learn from all of this. One: The longer you employ the power of compounding the better you offset the effects of inflation. Two: There are no good reasons to delay. The sooner you get started the better. You cannot change the past, so put any unproductive regrets behind you. Wherever you are, no matter how old you are, start putting the power of compounding to work for you at once. (More specifics on implementation will be given in the Master Plan in Section III.)

CHAPTER 10

Taking An Interest In Interest

One of the lovable characters from American folklore is Mark Twain's artful knave, Tom Sawyer. Well known is the episode when Tom has been assigned by his Aunt Polly to paint the fence, a task he does not relish. Indignant, he unenthusiastically begins the project of applying the paint by himself. Before long, however, Tom's keen mind develops a plan to extricate himself from the hands-on drudgery. He soon figures out a way of employing the labor of others, by conveying the impression that whitewashing a fence is some sort of a diversion. Within minutes, several of Tom's friends are enjoying all the fun of completing Tom's task for him. Young Mr. Sawyer winds up completing the task in a hands-free supervisory role. (Mark Twain may be credited with having written the first American management text.)

Two lessons can be absorbed from Tom Sawyer's methods. First, what constitutes "work" and what constitutes "play" is a matter of perspective. One person's work is another person's recreation. The second lesson is more applicable to our current topic. There are basically two ways of getting a job done: Do it yourself or employ the labor of others. When it comes to accruing a living income: You can work for money, but you can also put money to work for you. (There is a third choice, I suppose, but charity and welfare are untenable for most of us.) Ultimately, if you live long enough, not even the first choice will be an option. Those who do not learn how to put money to work for them will experience grim repercussions in their old age.

Through the metaphors of Arkad and Tom Sawyer I have drawn parallels to the power of compound interest. I have even used these figures to teach my children. I have noted the excitement as they catch the idea that every coin they save becomes a worker in their own "personal company." What is abstract to children, must become a practical reality to us adults. Our appreciation for the power of compound interest must not be shallow. The facets of this principle need to be thoroughly assimilated.

Let us continue our analysis by taking the example of a struggling college student, age 21, setting a modest monthly savings goal. Let us suppose she decides to begin saving $40 per month and plans to continue that simple habit right on through her college days until her retirement at age 65, a total of 44 years. While it might be a fairly significant sacrifice for the first few years, that sum would hardly be missed in the ensuing years. Again, over time the results are significant.

EXAMPLE NO. 1: $40 PER MONTH AT 10 PERCENT

	10 years	=	$8,196
	20 years	=	$30,094
	30 years	=	$99,893
	40 years	=	$246,773
At retirement	44 years	=	$368,661

Through a modest effort this student has appended to her retirement picture a noteworthy addition. Living on the interest on the accrued $368,000 from that point on, she would put an additional $30,000 per year into her living allowance.

EXAMPLE NO. 2: $100 PER MONTH AT 10 PERCENT

If you are beyond the age of 21, do not be disheartened. Just increase the monthly amount and apply the same principle. If, for example, you are in your early 30s, you would need to save $100 per month to achieve essentially the same result.

$$
\begin{array}{rcl}
20 \text{ years} & = & \$75,602 \\
25 \text{ years} & = & \$129,818 \\
30 \text{ years} & = & \$217,131 \\
35 \text{ years} & = & \$357,752
\end{array}
$$

In this example, at retirement you would again have accrued approximately a third of a million dollars and would enjoy the same $30,000 boon to your living allowance.

Through the power of compounding, even modest sums can grow into sizeable accumulations over the years. One hundred dollars from your budget would not alter your current lifestyle much, yet the long-range effect would be respectable.

If most people could just retire with an additional $350,000, making them a very reasonable $30,000 per year in non-compulsory income, their freedom and peace of mind would be markedly enhanced.

Our third example is more challenging, and may not be within the realm of reality for most earners, but, then again, who is to say? I include this example not to discourage you but in the hopes that it may inspire you.

EXAMPLE NO. 3: $10,000 PER YEAR AT 10 PERCENT

If you were to save $10,000 *per year* at 10 percent compounded annually for 30 to 35 years, you would reap these exciting yields:

Deposits	Total Accrued	Net effect	
10 years	$100,000	$175,312	
15 years	$150,000	$349,497	(Over 2 times the deposits)
20 years	$200,000	$630,025	(Over 3 times the deposits)
25 years	$250,000	$1,081,818	(Over 4 times thedeposits)
30 years	$300,000	$1,809,434	(Over 6 times the deposits)
35 years	$350,000	$2,891,268	(Over 8.5 timesthe deposits!)

Very few people retire with $3 million in liquid funds to their credit. Many dream of investing their way to that kind of wealth, but less than a fraction of 1 percent do so. Yet, there are many people who have the income which could bring that kind of results if they would simply apply a bit of consistent discipline.

THE SIGNIFICANCE OF THE COMPOUNDING PERIOD

When you open up a savings account of any type, it pays to be certain of the compounding interval. Some banks and credit unions compound *quarterly* and some compound *monthly*. Almost all institutions will compound your account monthly if you demand it. The difference is significant.

Let me just show you a side-by-side comparison:

$25,000 AT 10 PERCENT

Years	Annually	Quarterly	Monthly
5	40,263	40,965	41,113
10	64,844	67,127	67,676
15	104,431	109,995	111,348
20	168.187	180,239	183,202
25	270,868	295,343	301,424
30	436,235	483,954	495,935

The figures speak for themselves. I leave the conclusions to you.

THE RULE OF 72

There is a handy little rule which can help you make quick mental computations on the growth of your nest eggs. It is called the "Rule of 72," and it is a simple way of determining the time required to double your principal. To learn how long it will take to double your money at any given interest rate, simply divide 72 by the interest rate. The answer will be the number of years it will take to make one of your dollars become two. So, if you are earning 8 percent on your money, it will take you 9 years to double your money (72 / 8 = 9). Applying the same formula, if you are earning 10 percent on your money, it will take you a little over 7 years (7.2) to double your present principal.

ACCUMULATING A MILLION

Here is another way to visualize the miracle of compounding: What does it take to *save a million dollars*; that is, how much money would you have to put aside if your goal was to save $1 million? The answer depends on how much you want the resource of time and the power of compounding to assist you.

Let me show you. Let us suppose that you could get an annual interest rate on your money of 9 percent compounded monthly. Here is a sequence showing how much you would have to deposit monthly and how long it would take to achieve the goal. I am going to put this example in table form, but I am going to do so gradually, in order to emphasize the power of compounding.

YEARS	TOTAL PYMNTS	MONTHLY AMT
5	60	$13,258

In other words, if you wanted to save $1 million in 5 years you would have to save over $13,250 per month for the 60-month period. Now that is a lot. Not many could do that out of their own earnings. So, harness the power of consistency and a little patience and watch what happens. Continuing:

YEARS	TOTAL PYMNTS	MONTHLY AMT
10	120	$5,167
20	240	$1,497

By doubling the time frame, something interesting becomes evident. You reduce the amount you have to save by much more than half. Why? Because, you are making earnings on the earnings. Your first generation of "slaves" is begetting offspring who are now also working for you, and *both* generations are continuing to produce a larger *third* generation, which also works and begets. And so on; each generation becoming larger and more powerful. The process starts slowly, but it begins to "snowball" and with the passing of time, the momentum builds.

To show you how reasonable the goal can be, here is the rest of the table:

YEARS	TOTAL PYMNTS	MONTHLY PYMNT
25	300	$891
30	360	$546
35	420	$337
40	480	$211
45	540	$134

ANOTHER VIEW OF THIS PREMISE

There is another way of looking at this whole scenario which will also illustrate the power of compounding. I hope this will make a deep impression on your mind.

Using the self-same parameters described above, I want you to see how much of "your own money" is involved at the various plateaus.

At the end of each of these scenarios you wind up owning $1 million. The amount you had to actually *earn* by the "sweat of your own brow" is what I want to highlight for you.

YEARS	MONTHLY AMT	TOTAL AMT **YOU** DEPOSIT
5	$13,258	$795,501

In this case, you have saved $1 million and you have received some benefit from the compounding of interest, but not much. The net message here is that you had to earn and deposit the vast majority of those dollars yourself. You had only about 20 percent of your goal contributed by "slave labor."

If, however, you are willing to be patient, you can reduce your earnings burden significantly. Continuing:

GOAL: ACCUMULATE $1,000,000.

YEARS	MONTHLY AMT	TOTAL AMT YOU DEPOSIT
5	$13,258	$795,501
10	$5,167	$620,109
15	$2,642	$475,680
20	$1,497	$359,356
25	$891	$267,558
30	$546	$196,642
35	$337	$141,661
40	$211	$101,750
45	$134	$72,376

The power of compounding comes through loud and clear. In the case of the 30-year program, your slaves have accomplished over 80 percent of the work. The silent wonder in all of this is that you achieved the million dollar mark without a lot of worry, distraction or management on your part. You were not distracted and preoccupied with market fluctuations or crabby renters or the whims of consortiums and cartels.

In summary, becoming a millionaire is within the reach of anyone who really *wants* it. Save $900 per month at 9 percent (compounded monthly) for 25 years, for example, and you will achieve that notable goal.

THINK ABOUT IT

In my seminars, whenever there are some high school students in the audience, I invite a young man and a young woman up to the front of the group and offer them a deal. I ask them if they would be willing to give me $72,000 if I promise to give them $1 million in return. Not one of them has refused me yet. But, fortunately for me, to this date, not one of them has had the $72,000 cash either.

So I tell them I am going to "sweeten" the deal and make it easy on them. They can pay the $72,000 in installments, a little at a time. I ask them if they think the goal of having $1 million is worth a little (not a lot, but a little) work and sacrifice. Once again I receive, universally, affirmative answers. I then ask if their life really depended on it, could they earn and save $135 in the coming month. Usually I get a slight pause and then an affirmative answer.

"Could you do that again in the next month?" I continue.

"Yes," they respond.

"Then," I say, "Let's make the deal. You pay me $72,000 at a rate of $135 per month, and when you are done, I will give you $1 million." I say this as I am extending my hand as though to shake on the deal. Generally, they will pause and think about it for a moment.

As they pause, I ask them, "Are you hesitating because you think there is a catch? Do you wonder whether you can trust me or not?" Without letting them have a chance to answer, I say, "Well then just leave me out of this entirely. Do it *yourself*, because you do not need me. You can make this deal with yourself; that is the best way to do it anyway. Forget, Dennis Deaton. Just set up an account in a strong, solid institution and start this month, putting $135 in the bank each month at 9 percent, compounded quarterly, and you will be a millionaire before you hit retirement age. You will be richer than most doctors, or dentists, or lawyers when they retire, and you do not need luck or a middle-man." It gives them something to really think about (and the rest of the audience ponders it, too).

Before they leave the rostrum I follow one other line of questioning. I ask, "If you did save $135 this month and the next and then the next—consistently, month after month—which would be the hardest year?"

"The first," they respond.

"If you really wanted to do it, though, you could do it, right? I mean, if you really made up your mind, you could accomplish it even in what you consider to be the 'hardest year,' couldn't you?"

"Definitely," they answer.

"Would that habit get harder or easier, the older you got?" I query.

"Easier," they say.

"Why would it get easier?" I ask.

"Because we would have established the habit, and we will earn more per month as we progress. That $135 is a lot right now, but later on it will be practically nothing," is the essence of the responses I receive. I conclude the interview by confirming that statement with a warm assurance that I believe they are right—they *can* do it now, and if they will do it now, it will just get easier the older they get.

The fact is, for these young students, it will *never* be easier. The best time for them to start is *now*. At age 18 the road to financial prosperity is gradual and not overly taxing. The longer they wait, the steeper the journey will become. Yet the initial truth which applies to them applies to us all. The sooner we embark the better. The best time for you to commence—no matter your circumstance, no matter your age—is *now*.

THE BASIC COURSE

Robert Fulghum said, "All I really need to know I learned in kindergarten." (That is also the title of his book, an excellent book, by the way.) He points out that all of the basic requisites for happy, harmonious living were taught to each of us in the fundamental lessons of kindergarten. Kindergarten is a basic course in life management; and all we learn after that merely builds on the basic principles.

The same is true here. The basic principles of money management, the same principles advocated centuries ago, are the very principles we must build on today. There is wisdom in getting back to the basics.

The correct map for today actually redefines an old trail which was once an oft-used passage. Though the road is in disrepair and a bit overgrown from lack of use, the principles are solid and sound, and by using them in your map, you will arrive with certainty at a satisfying destination. The tried and time-proven pathway of the past is still the road to wealth.

CHAPTER 11

Calibrating The Course

No one stumbles onto financial freedom. It is not obtained through luck or some quirky stroke of fate. Financial freedom is a strategically planned ascent. It is the worthy reward bestowed only on those who seek it and apply the principles to merit and achieve it.

A strategic plan is an obvious requisite but that, in turn, presupposes a strategic vision. The clearer the view of the terrain and the more detail one is aware of, the more effective and accurate will be the strategic plan to negotiate a successful passage. Becoming money wise is the key to becoming "filthy rich."

The effect of inflation upon the dollar is one of the single biggest factors in your financial future. It is not possible to develop a clear and specific map until one sees and accepts this prominent element of the topography.

EDUCATION ON INFLATION

Beware. The road to financial freedom is an uphill climb. The terrain is very steep in many places. What is more, along the way, there lurks a wolf, and his name is Inflation. He is not a myth; he is real. We must accept this and realize he is not about to drop into a pot of boiling water so you and I can live happily ever after. Just because he is not always ranting about, wreaking havoc in plain view, does not mean he has left the scene.

We cannot naively pretend he isn't prowling about, and yet, at the same time, we cannot be overly fearful of him. It is not wise to cower, letting his howl in the moonlight affect our serenity at night nor our activities in the day.

Furthermore, we cannot run away from him. Nor should we follow the advice of the false map makers who tell us to invest our way around the ill-tempered beast. Instead, inflation must be faced and it must be dealt with.

Too many people *over-react*. Many false map makers use inflation as a means of lending authenticity to their ploys, scaring people into rash decisions and risky investments. (You may remember the warnings against such rash risk-taking in Chapter 5.) Such blunders actually exacerbate the harms the wolf can inflict. So, let's face the wolf. What is inflation and how big and bad is it?

A rose is a rose, but a dollar is not so constant. A dollar at the turn of this century is not the same as a dollar will be at the turn of the next. The dollar today does not have the buying power it once had. In the 30 years from 1956 to 1986, for example, the dollar experienced a 74 percent loss in value. In other words, in 1956, a dollar would buy *four times as much* as it would in 1986. In the early `60s, I remember that whole milk cost 49 cents a gallon. Today it is over $2. Whole milk is still whole milk. A gallon is still 128 fluidounces. It is the dollar which is different. It has diminished in purchasing power.

If the dollar has *diminished*, why do they call it *inflation*? The answer has to do with the law of supply and demand. The value of the dollar has deflated because the number of dollars has been inflated. The government has printed and put more money into circulation as compared to the value of goods and services, hence the value of the dollar as compared to these goods and services has fallen. Inflated numbers means deflated value.

Inflation is not new. Inflation has been around for centuries, and it appears it's here to stay. That is not necessarily bad. Almost all economists agree, a certain amount of inflation is actually healthy. Although they vary on how much is good and how much is bad, most concur that inflation is not inherently evil.

The core issue, the thing which matters most about inflation is the *RATE* at which the inflation is happening. During the 1950s, inflation averaged about 2 percent per year. The dollar lost value over that period of time, but the devaluation rate was low and the impact on purchasing power was gradual enough for adjustments to occur smoothly. In those days, people paid little attention to inflation. It did not start becoming a household word until the 1970s. In the first half of that decade, inflation rose over 6 percent per year and increased to nearly 9 percent in the latter half of that 10-year period. The *rate* of inflation had accelerated to the point where people actually realized their dollars were losing purchasing power. At the outset of the 1980s, when inflation hit 19 percent per year, people woke up. They were not getting as much per dollar, and they *knew* it. They could feel it at the grocery store, at the automobile dealership—everywhere they turned prices were sky-rocketing and their purchasing power was perceptibly dwindling.

This awakening had its good points. Most working people became cognizant of preparing more wisely for their retirement years. Perspectives about the number of dollars needed to retire changed. People realized they could not retire at today's values but had to give some forethought to future values. The ones who got caught in the vise were the unfortunate souls who retired in the early '60s with what was then an adequate monthly income. By the end of the '70s, most of them were in an uncomfortable and uncontrollable pinch. The number of dollars they were receiving was fixed, but the purchasing power was not. Every day they fell further and further behind. The government made some modest attempts to adjust the Social Security allotments through "cost-of-living" adjustments, but many of our elderly wound up in poverty. They now find themselves attempting to live on the number of dollars that once would have meant a royal income but today means destitution.

More fortunate are we who are still working. We can be more money wise. Most of our grandparents did not understand the erosive effect of inflation. We have been forewarned. Let us act wisely in accordance with this knowledge.

BEWARE OF INFLATION'S BITE

The best way to get a perspective of inflation's effect on your future is to look at the realities of retirement. Preparing for a comfortable retirement should not be our exclusive destination in life, but it must certainly be part of a correct map. So, let's take a serious look into the future. (For some of you, retirement may not be that far distant and for others it is already here. If that is the case, be sure to share with your posterity any corroborations you can offer to substantiate what I am saying.)

I have often been amazed at how many people have no idea in the world what it takes to retire comfortably. Even many in their fourth and fifth decades have never put a pencil to the matter. They just keep plodding along in some kind of "earning trance," expecting that retirement will sort of take care of itself. They never, until it is almost too late, ask themselves, "How much money will I need to live on when I retire?"

DEFINING YOUR COMFORT LEVEL

The way to start crystallizing the vision is to determine how many of *today's* dollars are needed to sustain the retirement lifestyle you envision. If you were retired today, how much money would you require to live *comfortably* each month?

One of the best ways to reach an accurate response to that question is to ask several people who are retired and have the level of lifestyle you envision. Make sure they also live in the part of the country where you plan to retire as that affects the picture a great deal. Cost of living, tax rates and housing costs vary throughout the country. You can retire more cheaply in North Dakota than you can in Southern California. You must *not* take a wild guess at this issue. It's an integral part of your education to get a solid, definite answer to this query. Ask around. Most retired people are reluctant to tell you how much they have in aggregate, what their sources are, and how much they have in savings, but most will be glad to honestly tell you what it costs each month to maintain their standard of living.

It will not hurt to also ask some people who live *below* your intended standard to see how many of today's dollars they are trying to manage on. That can also be very instructive.

Every person I have talked to who has conducted this survey has found it *very* enlightening and *very* meaningful. It has truly opened their eyes to the realities retired people face.

Below is a partial list of factors that you may consider as you think about what will constitute a comfortable lifestyle:

1. Do you intend to own your residence (or residences)?

2. Do you plan to own the home outright, or are you still planning to make mortgage payments, or do you plan to rent?

3. How much traveling do you plan to do?

4. How many cars and recreation vehicles are you going to own? What kind of transportation do you intend to have? How much does a new car in today's dollars cost? What about insurance and sales tax?

5. How much will health care and medical insurance cost? (That answer will really blow your mind.)

Suffice it to say, explore the issue carefully. Try to look through the eyes of several people, so you get an accurate picture. Inquire of single individuals and couples. When you get enough opinions, a definite answer will form in your mind and be confirmed.

Once that question is answered, you are ready to start projecting yourself forward in time to the days of your own retirement. The question naturally then becomes, "How many *future* dollars will you need to provide the lifestyle you are planning to enjoy?" The answer depends on two more questions:

1. How many years away is your retirement?

You need to take into consideration the amount of time there is between the present and your retirement years. Time is a factor because the value of the dollar is time dependent. Today's dollar has a certain buying power. However, as we have seen, that value is not fixed nor static. The dollar forges downward in value, year by year, as time marches onward. You will have to take the number of today's dollars and adjust that figure upwardly in order to maintain an equivalent standard of living. Logically, the further you are from retirement, the higher your adjusted figure must be, as you will soon see.

2. How much inflation will there be between the present and your retirement?

Unfortunately, there is no definite answer to this question. The correct answer is, *NOBODY* KNOWS. That is what makes the whole scenario so challenging. We can only estimate, and your guess is as good as anyone's. Professional economists and analysts try to predict the answer to this question and their batting average is not all that impressive. I will not try to guide your thinking too much, you need to come up with your own "wrong answer," because you are the one who has to live with the consequences.

Nothing is chiseled in stone anyway, you will have to make course adjustments along the trail. The key, for now, is to get a perspective.

To make your estimation process somewhat less ambiguous, let me give you a chart to show you what the recent history of inflation has been.

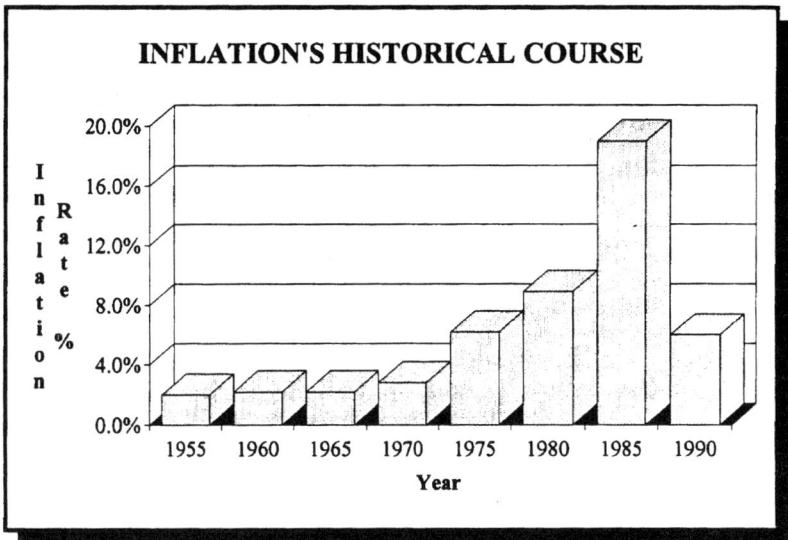

INFLATION'S HISTORICAL COURSE

I will also inform you that a very reputable financial group estimates the rate of inflation in the 1990s to be less than 5 percent annually. Others are not so optimistic and place the average at slightly over 8 percent. (Please note that these same entities were off significantly in the 1980s. At the outset of the '80s the rate of inflation was increasing steeply. These same august entities made forecasts which reflected that trend. They predicted inflation was going to continue to soar. It did not. Reaganomics (or Nancy's astrologer) produced a cooling effect on inflation and the *rate* of inflation declined. Most of the experts *overestimated* the rate of inflation.)

Now let us arbitrarily put in a rate just to show you how that may affect your thinking. This exercise is to give you perspective, not heart failure. Before I bring the Boogie Man out of the closet (the one starring in the hit horror film, "The Innocents Meet Retirement Reality"), I want to assure you and reassure you that the wealth plan in this book will bring you ample success.

Now for a brief appearance on stage by the Boogie Man: Let us suppose that, after performing your survey, you have come to the conclusion that at retirement you will own your dwelling. Owning your residence outright, you decide you will need $40,000 per year to live comfortably. That amount will cover your basic needs and will provide a sufficient number of frills to enjoy life. Let us further suppose that there is no Social Security, no retirement or pension income from any other source—your only income is the interest on your savings.

Your formula to compute the amount of principal needed to sustain yourself is:

$$\frac{\text{Annual Living Expense}}{\text{Rate of Return on Principal}} = \text{Amt of Principal Required}$$

Or, in other terms: If you need $40,000 per year and are making 8 percent per year on your savings, how big must the nest egg be?

Plugging in our hypothetical values, we get:

$$\frac{\$40,000}{8\%} = \$500,000$$

This means you would need to have, today, $500,000 gaining 8 percent per year to supply you with $40,000 per year to live on. Again, this is all in terms of today's dollars. Now let's factor in time and inflation.

A RETIREMENT EXAMPLE

If inflation is chugging along at a nice steady rate of 5 percent per year, then after a certain number of years, the money would be worth one half of what it is today. This is called the "half life of money." At a rate of 5 percent, the half-life of money is just over 14 years. (The Rule of 72 in reverse.)

This means that if inflation were to hold steady at 5 percent for the next century, then every 14 years the money would be worth half of what it was 14 years previously. Another way to look at the scenario is to visualize prices doubling every 14 years.

Let us take, as an example, a 23-year-old man who is planning on retirement at age 65. His envisioned lifestyle accords with the parameters depicted above—he owns his home and will need, 42 years down the road, the equivalent of 40,000 of today's dollars per year (or about $3333 per month). If he fails to factor inflation into the picture, he will be destitute on a $3333 per month income when he gets to be 65.

Here is why: There are essentially three 14-year intervals between age 23 and age 65. That means his purchasing power will be cut in half three times. Explicitly, 14 years from now, or when the man will be 37 years old, $3333 will purchase only half of what it does today. In other words, he would be getting by, in the equivalent of today's dollars, on only $1667. The succeeding 14 years double the damage. By the time the man has reached age 51, he would have to be managing on what would be in today's dollars $834. ($1667/2 = $834.) Eventually, in the final 14-year interval, just as he is reaching retirement age at 65, the man would have lost half of his purchasing power once again. The horror is straight out of a Stephen King novel. If our friend, 42 years from now has $500,000 in the bank, he would have to be getting by on what today is a paltry $417 a month. ($834/2 = $417) Now you see the macabre reality inflation and those 42 years bring into one's retirement picture.

Rushing to the point, (so we can get on to the good news) in order to have, 42 years from now, the standard of living that $40,000 per year would bring today, our young friend would have to have a principal balance considerably larger than $500,000. The rude truth is he would need 8 times that much or a tidy $4 million. (Go ahead, faint.)

RESTRAIN THY PANIC

There is no question about it, Virginia, the wolf is big and he is bad. Granting that as a given, let us not become overly wrought up in despair or panic.

Although that amount of money sounds like a fortune, things are not nearly as grim as they might first appear. There are going to be strong favorable forces at work in your behalf, off-setting inflation's effects. Some of these forces will occur almost naturally. Others you are going to set in motion yourself (by following the Master Plan outlined in Section III).

Before proceeding to that discussion, let us first complete the calibration of your personal course. Based on the discussion in this chapter, you should now be able to answer the following:

1. Number of years until retirement
    plus 5 =   (a)

2. Your estimate of the annual rate of
    inflation from the present until (a)=   (b)

3. Annual income (in today's dollars)
    you need at retirement =   (c)

Now, turn to the Table of Computational Factors denoted as Appendix A in the back of the book. Using the values selected for (a) and (b), locate the corresponding computational factor.

For example, if your estimate of the inflation rate (b) was 5 percent, and your years to retirement plus 5 equals 15, then the computational factor is 2.08.

The rest is simple. To determine the annual income required for your comfortable retirement, multiply the annual income in today's dollars (c) by the computational factor and there you have it!

FORMULA 1:

Comp. Factor   x   Today's Income =Estimated Annual Income
                                (c)   Required at Retirement

To complete the calibration process we need to have one other insight. What will be required to produce and sustain that level of income? If you have no other source of income—no Social Security, no retirement or pension income, no income from any assets other than your savings—this is what you would need to have salted away at retirement:

FORMULA 2:

Estimated Annual Income
Required at Retirement = Amount of Principal
Interest Rate On   Needed In Savings
Savings

In other words, if you estimate the going rate of interest for savings to be 8 percent at the time of your retirement, and your estimate of annual income needed came out to be $200,000, then the amount of principal needed in savings to sustain yourself would be $2.5 million. (Get the smelling salts, Edna!)

$$\frac{\$200,000}{8\%} = 2,500,000$$

This, for many people, is what you *really* call "Future Shock." You must keep reminding yourself that this is *tomorrow's* dollars, not today's. Much of the sting of this picture is going to be soothed by the fact that many of the aspects of inflation are also favorable to your assets, your income and your ability to save substantial amounts of money. Also, you are going to take other definitive steps to achieve a comfortable and secure future. The road ahead is clear and dry, I assure you. If you stay the course; things will work out.

The key to all of this is perspective. There are two perspectives I hope you will gain from this exercise. First, you must gain the perspective that looking into the future is a key part of becoming money wise.

We are taking the pains to compute these figures so you can become aware of what the future portends so that you can adequately prepare yourself. Expanding your perspective and enlarging your expectations of the future, you can move forward with confidence. There is a truth which my family and I hold dear, "If ye are prepared, ye shall not fear."

Second, I want you to get a perspective about the "Relativity of Money." It is hard to believe right now, but 25 years into the future an annual income of $200,000 will seem as ordinary and commonplace as an annual income of $45,000 does today. For those who are gainfully employed, inflation is not as harmful as for those on fixed incomes. During your lifetime, inflation has been eating away at the dollar, yet you have been able, relatively speaking, to keep apace. It is when you *stop* working and have to survive on a *fixed* income that inflation becomes so vicious. Being aware of that fact, allows you to implement the measures to insure happy days ahead even after you have ceased to earn a monthly salary.

ONE MORE PERSPECTIVE

There is one perspective which I do *not* want you to assume from the foregoing instruction. Financial freedom is not to be equated solely with "a comfortable retirement." I have cited this element of the financial picture for the purpose of giving you a clearer perspective about inflation and about compound interest. Each of us needs to appreciate future values of the dollar and the relativity of money as we design our individual maps. Those concepts are important components, but are not the comprehensive whole, and we must be careful not to *over*simplify.

I want you to see that time is *not* money as the adage alleges. Time is far more important than money and has power over the value of money. Viewing retirement in one's specific terms is simply the best way to bring those realities into focus. It is not, however, my intention to convey that financial success is synonymous with early retirement, no matter how luxuriously or opulently that goal can be furbished.

One cannot be financially free, in my opinion, without providing for one's future, but as important as that is, it should not be your sole purpose or your exclusive destination.

AUNT AGNES

Some experiences never fade in the memory. One of my most vivid recollections occurred shortly after my wife and I were married. We were of very modest means. (Actually, that is an euphemism. We were young and enthusiastic, but we were broke.) We were both employed and we rented a small apartment from a well-to-do woman, who we affectionately called Aunt Agnes. One evening after work, we sat chatting with our landlady and the subject of life and life's perspectives came up. Our wise friend took the opportunity to instruct two young pupils. Aunt Agnes told us of her marriage and the hopes and dreams she and her husband had held when they were young. She regaled us in her anecdotal narrative of their early years together. They were diligent and prudent people, she explained, and they set a goal to retire well. Agnes observed that, in essence, that was their *only* financial goal.

To retire well and be able to enjoy their golden years in comfort and happiness, they committed themselves to that goal and worked hard. They earned good money through the years and they selected a mutual fund and made substantial monthly investments. As the U.S. economy grew and prospered through the '40s and '50s, their dollars multiplied, and by the time they had reached mid-life, they had a luxurious retirement in the offing.

Then Agnes' husband died. In the prime of life, and only a decade or so away from their golden retirement years, he was gone. Agnes now lives in a comfortable home, drives a very nice car, dresses well and has not a financial care in the world. There is nothing wrong with that.

She is grateful that she and her husband planned and prepared for the future. She is thankful she is not in the straits that some of her peers (who are also widows) are in. Yet, she had a monumental point to impress upon my young bride and me: "Don't spend all your money on the future. Enjoy some of it now."

We had heard the adage, "Don't go barefoot all your life, so you can be buried in silk slippers," but Agnes instilled it in us. She explained, in retrospect, they had gone too far in their focus on retirement. That being their *only* financial goal, they deferred *all* their enjoyment.

She said they seldom took a trip, seldom took their money and went to dinner and a show, seldom spent much of their money on each other. It went to the necessities and to the children; then all the rest went into the retirement fund. Her words still echo, "There is more to life than just preparing for retirement."

Our kindly landlady made a great impression on us that evening, one we have been sincerely grateful for. We slipped into our little apartment that night clutching an important concept—
the real wealth in life is LIFE! One needs to enjoy and be grateful

for every day. Each day is just as precious as another. A balance must be maintained. One must, absolutely must, prepare for the future, but must *live* in the present.

Delayed gratification is a hallmark of mature and successful people, but even that virtue can be taken too far. Tomorrow should not take total precedence over today; a wholesome balance must be struck. Obviously, just as touching, and often more tragic, are the examples of the converse—those who have been woefully unprepared for the future. People who, like the grasshopper in the ancient fable of "The Grasshopper And The Ant," fiddle all their time and money away in their youth, experience grinding poverty and even degradation in their advanced age.

THE POINT

In the next chapter you are going to be instructed to make some decisions—judgments about destinations and checkpoints. In this and the preceding chapters, I have attempted to give you perspective. (Hereafter, once you have your decisions made, you will be supplied with techniques to realize them.)

The point to bear in mind, despite all the emphasis on destinations, is that, in the final analysis, financial freedom has a lot to do with the direction you are moving, and a *balanced* way of traveling.

CHAPTER 12

The Map

Perspectives in place, it is time to create the map—a specific, customized plan for getting from wherever you are now to where you want to be. A fair amount of input will come from the book, but you will be making the final decisions.

There is no one correct map suited to every person or family. Obviously the variables are myriad, and thus each person must develop his or her own map. There are common features in all the correct maps, for they are all built upon the same foundation of correct principles. Yet, the specific goals, time frames and amounts will be widely varied.

You are responsible for your own map. Only you have access to all the pertinent facts. Only you know your current status. Only you can say what you want out of life and how your money should be used. Furthermore, only you are able to supply the answers to questions like: "How far?" and "How fast?" These answers are an integral part of formulating the concrete plan for your journey. However, as expressly recommended, you must first define your ultimate objective. This long-range destination serves as the reference point for orienting your map. Analogous to the North Star to navigators, it unifies all your efforts. Pick a future point in time and describe what you want life to be like when you get there. When it comes to money, what are your real purposes? What are your "ultimate monetary goals?" What does financial freedom actually mean to you?

It is important to get beyond the platitudes. Do not generalize. Imbue your vision with specificity and detail. Determine *exactly* how much you want to accumulate—by when and in what form. Put it in writing.

You may not find this such an easy assignment. Many people have a difficult time visualizing and projecting themselves forward in time. (I have encountered many who struggle with this in the classes I teach on the subject.) It is harder still to be specific and extensively detailed.

If an ultimate destination eludes you for the present, leave it for a while. Further on in the book some insights will be triggered which will clarify your thinking and elicit some ideas. You may want to read the book completely through once before you sit down to crystallize your vision and create your map.

For many people, a good place to start is with the answers obtained from Formulae 1 and 2 in the previous chapter, Chapter 11. What numbers did you come up with? How much do you need to accumulate to achieve the expected level of consistent, non-compulsory income? How are you going to generate that level of income?

PREDICTING FUTURE INCOME AND ASSETS

You have learned what inflation does to future purchasing power. The question now is, what will it do to your income and your assets? This is even more difficult to estimate because the variables are multiplied. To simplify, let us use percentages and current national averages. (There is no guarantee these will apply in the future, but it is the best we can do.) Seeing the picture today casts at least some light on the future.

Those people, today, who are totally dependent on Social Security for their income are impoverished. They are literally at the poverty level or below. By comparison, those retired people in the United States who are reasonably comfortable exhibit an income profile more along these lines:

Retirement Income Profile

Social Security 15-25%

Retirement Plan or Trust 40-60%

Dividend and Interest Income 25-40%

The people represented in this profile have prepared themselves better. Through an employer-funded or individually-funded retirement plan, they are deriving the bulk of their retirement income. Additionally, in liquid funds, they have savings which generate approximately one-third of their income.

Further up the scale, those who are in a stronger financial position are less dependent on Social *Security*. They are virtually self-sufficient. They live almost entirely on their dividend and interest income.

The foregoing is an extremely simplified statistical profile. It is presented to you for orientation purposes only. It should be clear, but apparently it is not; Social Security is a misnomer. It is unnerving how many people, even today, think that Social Security will take care of them in their old age. I beg you to exercise better judgment than they. At best, Social Security should be expected to provide 25 percent of your income, and possibly not even that.

Only you can make that call for yourself, but you had better give it some thought. How much do you want to depend on the government? Is Social Security going to be around at all? If it is, what portion of your income will it provide? What will Congress have to do to keep it solvent when the "Baby Boomers" hit retirement in massive forces? Will the succeeding generation be willing to foot the bill? No one can say for sure. The indefinite-ness of the future is, again, what makes the issue of financial planning so challenging.

The same investigation should be conducted of your company's retirement plan. Does your company or your employer have a retirement plan? How much will that provide you at retirement? What percentage of your income will be derived from that source? How safe is the plan? How financially well-grounded is your firm and its plan? Is it insured? Are you vested now and at what percent? All these questions must also be answered in order to define your destination.

If you are self-employed, have you established a qualified retirement plan? Is providing an ample retirement for yourself considered a standard part of your costs of doing business? Is the retirement fund being fully funded *every* year?

You get the idea. Think; and think in future terms as you define your long-term objectives.

In summary, it is imperative that you decide the following in regard to the long-range destination:

1. A specific date.

2. An annual income level in terms of that date.

3. The sources in percentages from which that income will be derived.

This gives you a *long-range* point of reference—a desti-nation which represents a culmination point. It specifies where you are going and demarcates when you have arrived.

CHECKPOINTS, CHARLEY

"Every great journey begins with a single step," states a Chinese proverb. Herein is timeless wisdom. Greatness is not achieved all at once. It comes incrementally, a step at a time.

No matter where you presently find yourself on the jour-ney to financial freedom, take this concept to heart. It is especially powerful if your present situation looks rugged and bleak. In such straits your worst enemy is discouragement and your greatest ally is faith and confidence. You will reinforce your enemy if you look at the journey as one giant step. It can seem to be overwhelming or even impossible.

Conversely, nothing is impossible to a faith-filled, committed human being, especially if the task is broken down into modest, believable subdivisions. Once your long-range map is defined, subdivide your journey. Do not try to get to Utopia all at once. Identify discrete checkpoints along the way, and chart your course to them one by one—one intermediate checkpoint at a time.

If you are one of the lone and weary travelers, stranded on some desolate detour, there is hope. But, don't be over-anxious. Breathe through your nose and take it in phases. You should consider a set of intermediate objectives I will offer, for the sake of example, a series of checkpoints. These are generalities at best and do not apply to all people in all walks of life. They may trigger some thoughts for you and that is my intent. The following will serve as a starting point as you make decisions about your personal set of checkpoints.

Checkpoint I:

1. Commit to living on less than you earn.

2. Commit to a disciplined savings program.

3. Commit to a debt elimination plan.

Checkpoint II:

1. Continue with defined budget.

2. Accumulate savings/retirement reserves of $50,000.

3. Pay off all debts, except for principal dwelling.

Checkpoint III:

1. Continue with defined budget.
2. Total Debt Liberation. No debts. Own your home.
3. Accumulate savings/retirement reserves of $100,000.

Checkpoint IV:

1. Continue with defined budget, and no debt.
2. Accelerate savings/retirement reserves to $500,000.
3. Diversify accumulated funds:

    a) Certificates of Deposit

    b) Money Market Mutual Funds

    c) Single Premium Deferred Annuities

(More information on diversifying your accumulated funds is provided in Chapter 19.)

Subdividing your map into phases, taking a segment of the journey at a time, you will get farther, faster. The accomplishment of each phase will bring a host of benefits. You reinforce your confidence and self-esteem. Your ability to deflect fear and discouragement will increase. As those counter-productive forces are surmounted, your mind becomes more focused. Creative ideas flow. Money accumulates, and its rate of accumulation increases. The pace of your overall progress accelerates.

OTHER BENEFITS

Getting yourself back on the road to accumulation will take commitment and effort. I assure you it is worth it. Your reward will come in several ways. You will extricate yourself from debt. Savings will accrue, and stress will abate. Most importantly, you will grow and be a stronger, more competent human being.

Money, in a broader perspective, is a most interesting resource. It can, like nothing else on earth, help human beings develop character. Most people use it to do precisely the opposite, but it does not have to be that way.

Personal traits such as industry and thrift, create wealth. But the means outvalue the ends. What you can obtain, intrapersonally, along that road outweighs what you can obtain when you get there. The personal strength that comes as you implement the principles is wealth you *can* take with you because it is what you have become. (Everything else is dust and stays here.)

A significant point to be understood is that wealth is a checkpoint along the road to financial freedom They are not synonymous terms. Character begets wealth but not necessarily financial freedom. Wealth, in a certain sense, tests the character, and when the test is passed, financial freedom is bestowed. This reward follows quickly and without exception. Once the lessons have been learned and mastered, the diploma is awarded lavishly and without delay.

A REWARD BEYOND THE RESULTS

There is one thing which has, above all else, become clear to me. There is much more going on in the world, particularly with the issue of money, than meets the mortal intellect. Value systems differ. It is safe to say that no two persons have precisely and exactly the same set of values. Not even two people who share a successful marriage can claim total congruity. To me, there are three central purposes for money:

1. TO PROVIDE THE RESOURCES FOR AN AMPLE LIVING:

To secure the basic needs of food, clothing and shelter, along with sufficient resources to develop talents and gain knowledge during the growth years.

2. TO PROVIDE A SECURE AND COMFORTABLE RETIREMENT:

To ensure an independent and dignified living in advanced age. To not be a burden on family or society.

3. TO INCREASE AND ENHANCE ONE'S CAPABILITY OF RENDERING SERVICE:

To allow time and means for employing one's mind and time to something *OTHER* than the providing of objectives 1 and 2. Money can be to used to free oneself from the pursuit of money. However, the more I ponder that issue, the more I start to see a larger purpose—something that I feel transcends our finite frame of reference.

As I introspected on my own weaknesses when I was mired in very uncomfortable financial plights, trying to discern what had gone wrong and what I needed to correct, I glimpsed something. As I analyzed people who had achieved wealth, and saw among them an even more elite group—people who had achieved something higher than wealth—people who possessed genuine financial freedom, I glimpsed it again.

As I studied and pondered the whole issue, as well as the purposes for money, something significant began to distill in my mind and the clearer I could see it. People who had achieved genuine financial freedom were different. They were patient, and they were in control.

These rare folks looked at time as an ally and were not in a hurry to revel in "the good life." They were willing to put correct principles to work and reap the benefits that time and concerted effort would bring. I am convinced that is *why* they succeeded. It was not so much due to their tactics, though, as what those tactics brought out or created or amplified in the people themselves. I began to understand that there was something bigger and more important going on at the center of it all. Their freedom was more of a reward than a result.

All my life I have believed in cause and effect relationships. I still do, and yet, there is more to it all than that. Every law which is applied yields a specific effect. It is a basic law of the universe. Would it be such a stretch of the imagination to believe that when certain laws are obeyed that in addition to the effect there is also a reward appended?

The men and women who had attained what I classify as genuine financial freedom possessed and enjoyed something beyond what "the effect" of their efforts would accord them. They, through patience and effort, had developed a set of personal, internal qualities—character, stamina and self-discipline. In turn, those qualities had brought them wealth as an effect, but they had something beyond the wealth. They had a total freedom of mind about money and material concerns and *that* had come more as a reward than as a result. It was as though it had been bestowe l on them rather than being something they had obtained as a resu t of their efforts, no matter how noble.

APPLICATION IS UP TO YOU

From this point on, and throughout the Master Plan, I will leave many of the application decisions totally up to you. How you want to employ the recommendations and principles will be at your discretion. What will be taught can serve numerous purposes and ends. It is a formula for money, the way back onto the road to accumulation and wealth from wherever you are now—stranded or just starting out. It is a formula for personal strength, character and increased power of self-discipline. It is also, I believe, a formula for infinitely more.

SECTION III

THE PLAN

You do not find until you seek.

There are two indispensable qualities which characterize successful men and women: Vision and Discipline. They see what they need to do; and then they do it. The previous two sections have supplied you with the vision of what to do. You must now move from the map to the journey. Section III is the Financial Freedom Master Plan. It teaches you how to get on the road to financial freedom from wherever you are now, and stay there. It will supply you with practical methods of obtaining the consistency and discipline to implement your map and *own* your money.

Own A Positive Mind Set

The master of money owns a positive mind set. I am not talking about some amorphous positive outlook towards life, some non-specific, cheery, "have-a-nice-day" attitude. I am talking about something that far surpasses weak-minded wishing. I am talking about WELL-FOCUSED COMMITMENT. I am talking about a specific, clearly defined, sharply focused objective which has crystallized into a total, positively unshakable tenacity—something that will not wilt when pain occurs or pressure mounts. I am talking about the type of personal, internal resolve that is so deep and so firm that behavior does not waiver. It is not allowed to. I am talking about exerting mental muscle.

Bluntly stated, most of us are mental weaklings. We have developed precious little capacity for self-discipline. We are so easy on ourselves that we have become mentally soft and morally anemic. Instead of developing character, we have developed extensive powers of rationalization. I overhear people every day making excuses and justifying their mediocrity. Only occasionally do I run across someone who does not—someone who refuses these self-deceptive practices.

NOT HYPE; SUBSTANCE. NOT WISHES; COMMITMENT

Not long ago, I had an appointment with a gentleman whose reputation for achievement in his field is virtually legendary. I had wanted to meet and get to know him because I had heard so much about him. Several people, accomplished and respected in their own right, had brought this man's name to my attention, stating that he was a genuine example of a self-disciplined person.

When I arrived at his office, he was just concluding a dialogue with one of his young administrative assistants. As soon as this young man departed and I was invited to sit down, my host looked across the desk and stated, "If people would just quit whining, and grab their problems by the throat and attack them, they could make 10 times the progress!" That is not your typical introduction, but I knew instantly that it was going to be a stimulating interview. (And I wasn't disappointed.)

Explaining what precipitated that comment, my host briefly described how his assistant had made a commitment, but things had not gone as expected. Now he was rationalizing and looking for ways to renegotiate the commitment. My new friend went on to state, "If he would just let the commitment stand—quit trying to wriggle out of it, and just go to work, he would succeed, and what is more, he would be stronger and better for it."

As we conversed, exchanging ideas and experiences, I was strongly impressed with the forceful mind set of this individual. It was not just what he said, it was how he said it. There was an authenticity in his personal integrity which I have not often seen.

Now that you have an idea of this man's character, I also wish to add that he is extremely well-to-do financially. He is "filthy rich" by almost anyone's standards. I hold that there is a direct link—a cause and effect relationship—between his character and his monetary success.

SOMETHING MONUMENTAL

"People have to learn to keep promises and commitments," he said. He continued, "I don't dare *not* keep my promises—whether to myself or another person. There is no difference, really. Every lapse weakens your character, and makes it that much harder to conquer the next rationalization. Before you know it, you have rationalized yourself into mediocrity, or worse."

I was impressed with how seriously, how almost sacredly, this man viewed the subject of commitment and promise-making. He seemed to be an anachronism—chronologically out of place— the last vestige of a defunct era in history.

There was a time when a person's word *was* a binding contract. Back then people did not make promises, contracts or commitments lightly—they thought about them, carefully. Once made, those pacts were ever-binding. Contracts were not made to be broken for gain, or expediency, or simply for convenience, as is so often the case in today's world. Technical loopholes, through which one might squirm, were totally beside the point. They were personally untenable—even reprehensible or repugnant. This interview gave me much to think about. It became lucidly clear to me that strong moral fiber is *not* the relic of some by-gone era. It has been and ever will be the pathway to genuine success and riches. Although not widely practiced today, it still stands as the common trait in every truly great man and woman.

Keeping everyday promises is something very meaningful, even crucial. Few habits build character and personal power like the one embodied in three simple words: KEEP *EVERY* PROMISE.

As I pondered this first blinding flash of the obvious, it led to yet another: THERE IS NOT ONLY POWER *IN* COMMITMENT, BUT THERE IS POWER *FROM* COMMITMENT.

Make no mistake about it. There is something very definite and very real that takes place inside you every time you keep a promise. It strengthens you. It adds power. You expand your capacity to accomplish bigger and better things. Each promise kept adds, and each failure subtracts. It is a simple and proportionate equation. The greater and more difficult the commitment, the greater the degree of empowerment when it is fulfilled. Keeping great promises brings great rewards, but no promise is too small or insignificant that keeping it won't add to one's personal reservoirs of strength.

In the final analysis, the determinant in life's battles is not complex: Strong people win; weak people lose. It is just that simple. And, in practical terms, one's strength is a function of how well one keeps covenants and promises.

MONEY IS A METER

Money can be a valuable tool in the process of learning to keep your promises. To me, that is one of the greatest things money can do for a person. In a certain sense, money is the *measurement system* on the road to self-mastery. It can help you gauge, day by day, your progress in acquiring personal power.

The wisdom of grandparents is a marvel. I had a grandmother who translated many of life's complex issues into simple terms. When I was a boy, she taught me:

> You have mastered yourself when you can hear something bad about another person, and not spread it; when you can receive injury or insult, and not return it; when you can have money in your pocket, and not spend it.

The hardest of the three may well be the last. I am thoroughly convinced that one's ability to control money is a clear barometer of one's level of self-discipline. For many it is the ultimate test. I have seen hundreds of people who can control every appetite and passion, who can comply with lofty standards of conduct in every aspect of life, but who are totally out of control when it comes to the issue of money. They cannot bring themselves into compliance with correct financial principles. They are poor, indeed.

My grandmother went on to say, "You can tell a lot about a person's character by how they earn their money, and how they use it."

Again, when it comes to money, there is no substitute for discipline. And when rightly viewed, *the converse is also true*: When it comes to discipline there is no substitute for money. The two go hand in hand.

If you want to become a strong, competent human being, master correct monetary principles. If you want to obtain and retain large sums of money, master correct self-management principles. You can look at it either way, building one builds the other.

THE FIRST STEP IS MIND MANAGEMENT

There is a simple reason why the first act in the Master Plan focuses on creating a positive mind set. None of the other acts will work until you have firmly made up your mind to apply them.

Make up your mind, here and now, that you are going to do it. Make a deep, abiding covenant to bring yourself into compliance and get tough with yourself. Giving in to oneself at the slightest twinge of pain is the singular hallmark of the mediocre and the financially strapped. The powerful concepts in the remainder of this book will bring you freedom, success and high self-esteem only when you put them to work for you. A firm commitment to do so must become your dominant thought.

When you exert control of your mind—*discipline your dominant thoughts*—the behavior, accomplishment and achievements take care of themselves. Behavior is mind driving body in fulfillment of dominant thought. Thoughts are the precursors of every action and every achievement. A basic tenet of life is, "as you sow so shall you reap." Nowhere does that hold more true than in the garden of the human mind. Every dominant thought is a seed which germinates into the corresponding action. Whatever we do, we do first in our minds.

Here is one way to ensure an effective mind set: Create a few "Strategic Signposts." It is not good enough to know the map is here in this book or written down in a notebook somewhere. You have to see it—think about it—several times each day. Every highway has its share of signs and billboards. I suggest you take control of the ones on your road to financial freedom by positioning copies of the Accumulation Map in strategic locations.

Take several 3-by-5 cards and list these essential ideas:

*1 THE GOAL IS **ACCUMULATION**, NOT JUST ACQUIREMENT.

*2 THERE ARE ONLY TWO LAWS OF ACCUMU-LATION:

    1. Don't Spend All I Earn.

    2. Don't Lose What I Save.

*3 A PART OF ALL I EARN IS MINE TO KEEP:

    1. Pay Myself First.

    2. Pay Myself At Least 10 Percent Each Month.

    3. Let My Savings Compound.

Underline the parts that will reinforce the concepts most emphatically to your mind. Place these signs in strategic locations, so as you go through the day, your thoughts will return to your commitment and reinforce it.

Post one of your signs on the mirror where you shave or apply your make-up, one on the dashboard of your car, one on the door of the refrigerator, one on your desk, one on the inside cover of your organizer or planner, and, maybe most importantly, one on the cover of your checkbook. The consistent repetition will pay large dividends and will open the door to the rest of the Master Plan.

One more suggestion: Don't just read the signs...Think! The signpost technique works well, but you have to keep breathing fresh air into it, or it will become stale and ineffective. After a few weeks, the signposts may become familiar and commonplace. To overcome this pitfall, change the cards occasionally. Put them in a different position on the mirror—the upper left corner, instead of the right, for example. Change the color of the card and/or the style or form of the writing. Just taking the time to replace and reposition the signposts every two or three weeks will reinforce the map. As you rewrite or retype new cards you will be reinstating the concepts. Make the map a dominant thought, and major improvements will result.

A SECOND TECHNIQUE

A second way to strengthen your commitment and build your mind set is "Verbalized Affirmation." This technique is especially effective for couples, although it can also work on an individual basis, as I will explain later.

Since in many circumstances you are seeking financial freedom with another person, both partners must be totally committed to the objectives. The mind set must be jointly shared. In some relationships this is a major obstacle. The partners do not communicate well and the issue of money separates them even further. The following technique can help overcome that. It fosters communication as the verbalized commitment of each partner reinforces and empowers the commitment of the other.

I know from personal experience this technique works. Until this objective became a firmly entrenched mind set, my wife, Susan, and I would hold a simple, daily "commitment session." At the beginning of each day, we would pause for a moment, look one another in the eye, and hold a "one minute pep rally." I would start. "A part of all we earn is ours to keep," I would say to her. In turn, looking firmly into my eyes, she would say, "A part of all we earn *is* ours to keep." I would respond with, "Yes!

A part of all we earn is *ours* to keep! We will not spend all we earn. We will not lose what we save." And she would reaffirm, "Yes! A part of all we earn is ours to *keep*! We will not spend all we earn! We will not lose what we save! We are going to ACCUMULATE, not just acquire!"

This may seem peculiar to you, but it worked wonders for us. It proved to be an effective way to maintain the intensity of our mutual commitment. It got us through our moments of weakness when we were tempted to splurge or deviate from the objectives of the map.

We found it especially important to do this on Monday mornings. Getting back into the harness of the work week, we prepared our minds to be successful in following the Accumulation Map. Before launching into our pursuits, we reminded ourselves *why* we were going our separate ways. It was not just to acquire and spend. Breaking even was not good enough anymore. We reminded ourselves that we were going to *win* this week—to gain some ground on our financial dreams.

In effect, we were looking each other in the eye and promising each other that at the end of month we would own more money than we did at the beginning of the month.

From small means were great things accomplished. We got tough. We worked on our weaknesses. Gradually, over a period of weeks, we got stronger. Our spending stayed in check; the objectives of the map became governing forces in our lives. Our savings began, for the first time, to grow—really grow, not just bob up and down, as we would put a little in and, a short while later, draw it out again. We learned to achieve consistency.

If you are single, this technique can still work for you. Once a day, stand in front of a mirror, look yourself directly in the eye, and affirm the map. Say it out loud. Repeat it at least twice. Get into it. Affirm the concepts with conviction and certitude.

Make up your mind, once and for all, that you are going to get mentally tough—stop pampering yourself—and become strong and financially free.

TWO HEADS, ONE PURSE

There is an unexpected and very significant by-product that can come into a marriage because of the Verbalized Affirmation technique. The key word in the rally is the word "our." Money can be the issue which divides a couple or it can strengthen the relationship. Often the spouse who is doing the earning implies that money is more "mine" than "ours." (After all whose name is on the paycheck anyway?) In subtle ways an atmosphere of distrust is created. Even in two-check relationships the feeling of "mine" and "yours" frequently exists, and is an unabashed detriment. Abolish that type of thinking.

When an earner implies, "This is the money that I earned. Be careful how you spend it," a lethally destructive seed has been planted. Here and there, the earner conveys resentment over expenditures by the other. The spender resents being resented. Soon the money becomes a wedge which divides the two. When the message, "I cannot trust *you* with *my* money," starts seeping into a marriage, the bell has begun to toll.

The daily "pep rally" effectively reverses that tide. It reaffirms that yours is a partnership, that it is *our* money. Who actually earns it is not an issue. You live together. You sustain one another in myriad ways beyond matters of money. You are a team. Neither could accomplish as much without the love and support of the other. By melding all of your resources, tangible and intangible, you are going to go farther and higher than either could go alone.

For Dennis and Susan Deaton, the daily confirmation session became a bonding force that welded us together, stronger than ever before. It augmented and heightened TRUST. In our case, I am the only one who works outside the home. As I looked into Susan's eyes and said, "A part of all we earn is ours to keep," she knew she could trust me to work hard and smart in order to maximize the income.

As she returned the commitment, I knew she was going to do her utmost to manage the household resources wisely. I could count on her. She could count on me. We were committed to each other and to our mutual goals, and we were reassured of that daily. Trust was fortified. This empowering element of the technique is something we just stumbled on to. We did not foresee these benefits at the outset.

THE GREAT POWER OF SMALL DIFFERENCES

Through our own experiences, Susan and I rediscovered some golden nuggets of wisdom (and we weren't even prospecting). Sometimes it is just simple thoughts and modest methods which produce enormous differences. Inspired teachers throughout the annals of history have drawn our attention to these two truths:

1. GREAT THINGS SPRING FROM SMALL BEGINNINGS, and

2. BY SIMPLE MEANS ARE GREAT THINGS ACCOMPLISHED.

The "Great Oak and the Acorn" and the "Parable of the Mustard Seed" are well-known examples. From modest beginnings and through simple means is greatness achieved.

From the invisible precursor of a correct mind set and firm commitment, you will grow to a position of wealth and financial freedom. You can do what others have done; the people who are money wise and "filthy rich" have emerged from modest beginnings by employing simple means.

From silent, internalized commitments—from crystal clear visions coupled with covenants in the mind—come *all* worthy achievements.

CHAPTER 14

Own A Savings Plan

If I could pass on *only one sentence* of financial advice to my children, it would be: *OWN* A SAVINGS PLAN. That habit paves the way to every other positive financial accomplishment. Learn to pay yourself first. Your "wages" should not be less than 10 percent per month, no matter what your earnings. Establishing a consistent, disciplined, monthly savings habit is imperative.

Saving money is a potent antidote against Prospector's Mentality. It endorses accumulation over mere acquirement. Furthermore, when compared to how well the average person fares in the arenas of speculation, it may well be, the *best* way to accrue real, tangible growth on your money. The vast majority of "investors" come to discover (when all the bobbing and weaving is over) a stark truth: they would have been miles ahead, if they would have just kept it simple. Their savings do more for them than all the "investment" contortions they put themselves through, and saving is decisively less stressful.

The experience of another good friend of mine is illuminating. Successful and prosperous, he is a real gentleman and I enjoy our relationship. (He and his wife throw some of the greatest gourmet dinner parties you would ever care to attend.)

Seeking to multiply his earnings, he had, over the years, ventured into numerous fields of "investment." During his lifetime he had owned stocks and bonds. He had purchased treasury bills. There had even been a fling with gold, silver and diamonds. He had been a limited partner in a couple of small business ventures. He had also invested in his share of real estate—his pride and joy being a lovely ranch in Wyoming. That led to "investment" (speculation) in livestock and related matters. In short, he has had his finger in just about every mainstream investment pie in America.

I vividly recall a conversation we had one day. To my friend of broad investment experience, I posed the question, "What is the best financial investment you have ever made?"

He did not answer quickly. He thought about it for a few minutes, then responded, "You know, it's interesting. About six or seven years ago, my wife and I decided to set aside $500 a month from our budget into savings. We are good about it, and we have discovered we hardly miss that money. It doesn't seem to alter our lifestyle much. Each month we just put $500 in a passbook savings account until we accumulate $5000. Then we roll it into a CD (Certificate of Deposit). We have kept that going with a fair amount of consistency."

My friend summed up with a salient remark, "You know, to be totally honest with you, WE HAVE DONE BETTER WITH THAT SIMPLE PROGRAM THAN ANY INVESTMENT WE HAVE EVER GOTTEN INTO." His next statement was also very meaningful. He said, "By the time you figure everything into most of my investments—the commissions coming and going, the expenses and payments, the legal fees, the accountant fees, the taxes, and so on, I've never made any REAL money in any of those other things. Most of the time, I've actually lost a little. I'm really not what you would call a successful investor."

He was being open and honest, and I appreciated his candor. He may not be a successful investor, but he is a *typical* one.

The truth is, most investors do not make money when all is said and done. They lose. Some lose a little. Some lose a lot.

Play the game if you will, but sooner or later you will come to understand the tremendous power of just keeping it simple: Master a Savings Plan! OWN IT!

THE RESERVOIR PRINCIPLE

In the western states there is an ingenious system of water repositories called reservoirs. When the pioneer homesteaders came to these arid lands, they encountered notable differences in the climate from that they had known in the eastern river valleys. The territory was parched and the rainfall was sparse, sporadic and unpredictable. In Arizona, where I live, things are more predictable—there is *never* much rainfall.

To sustain crops and livestock, and make communities possible, the early pioneers went up into the mountains and dammed off the flow of streams and rivers and created lovely man-made lakes. These reservoirs offered much to the people in the valleys below, and they still do. They are places of beauty. They are places of recreation—fish and wildlife flourish because of their existence. They are also reservoirs of security and peace of mind. For, in the summer, when the rain is slight, the water stored in the reservoirs is piped to the valleys and life goes on. Herein is a great symbol, and it does not take a quantum physicist to see it. Monetary reservoirs offer the selfsame benefits as water reservoirs. You can create for yourself and your family some monetary reservoirs—some lakes of liquid financial security.

The principles for creating reservoirs are remarkably comprehensible. When outflow *equals* inflow you have "river." When outflow is *greater than* inflow you have "drought." When outflow is *less than* inflow you create "reservoir." The longer inflow exceeds outflow, the larger the reservoir becomes. Now note this: Once the reservoir has been established, outflow can be equal to inflow, and the reservoir will remain. The reservoir stays and so do all of the attendant joys and benefits.

This unambiguous metaphor also deftly illustrates one of the original distinctions made at the outset of the book. It can be applied to visualize the difference between acquirement and accumulation. Those who focus only on acquirement are confusing the rain with the reservoir. To achieve the benefits I have described and alluded to, you must do more than make it rain hard once in a while. You must implement ways of *collecting* and *conserving* that rainfall.

THE PRINCIPLE OF CYCLES

Virtually every living thing grows by passing through systematic patterns called cycles. There is a regularly recurring sequence of events which takes the organism from one stage of development to another. The perennial cycle of plants is a classic example. Every year the cycle repeats itself, rhythmically and inexorably, adding to or subtracting from the growth of previous years. Each annual cycle (micro-cycle) is a subset of yet another broader cycle—the overall Life Cycle (macro-cycle) of the organism itself.

The pattern of cycles is everywhere. It is a governing force in all living things. Mankind is not exempt. However, there is one difference in the cyclical growth of human beings. Much of the growth in our stages of development is discretionary. There is a fair degree of agency associated with our cyclical trends. We make the choices, choosing whether our cycles ascend or descend. Our life becomes the product of the micro-cycles of our own device.

Most of us intuitively sense this truth. Near the end of each year, we become contemplative and introspective. We evaluate our lives and progress. We mull. We assess. Comparing one year's accomplishments to another, we discern trends of progression or retrogression. People who excel act on those comparisons. They *make sure* the current micro-cycle expands and increases, knowing that it is not just this one increment which is at stake but the expanded potential for an even greater growth in the micro-cycle to come.

The Principle of Cycles focuses our attention on a familiar, time-vindicated truth: You are in competition with no one but yourself. You compete with yourself in making each annual cycle as effectual and significant as possible.

COMBINING THE POWER

Monitoring personal progress in terms of yearly cycles, then, becomes a significant issue *and a significant tool*. In combination with other principles, the forces can be momentous. I now offer you a method of markedly accelerating the growth of your savings reservoir which combines the power of three potent forces:

1. Annual Cycle

2. Internal Competition, and

3. The Power of Simple Means.

This combination can be explosive. I have seen dozens of astounding examples which are nothing short of stunning.

A METHOD OF ACCELERATION

First, *keep a Savings Journal*. From this point on, maintain a record of your savings activity. This provides a fulcrum upon which great self-disciplinary leverage can be applied. Form

4555 is an example of an effective savings journal. (An illustration of this form is shown on the next page.)

Next, subscribe to the following:

A DECLARATION OF INDEPENDENCE

1. I WILL ACCUMULATE MONEY. Not assets. Not possessions. Money.

2. I WILL ACCUMULATE MONEY *EACH MONTH*. No exceptions. I will not allow a month to go by without moving forward to a higher level of wealth. Each month brings me more money. Some of it is mine to keep. At the end of each month, I will own more money than I did at the first of the month.

3. I WILL KEEP A RECORD. I will keep score. I will keep a savings journal. For the rest of my life, I will record how much I add to my reservoir of wealth each month.

4. I WILL COMPARE. I will measure myself against myself. Each month's achievements will be matched with the previous year's achievement for the corresponding month (and will eventually be compared with the past several years' achievements).

5. I WILL COMPETE. I will *surpass each month's record* of the previous year. Each month will be a new "lifetime record." Each annual cycle of my life will not only find me further ahead, but stronger. Each year my progress shall not only be greater, BUT MY *RATE OF PROGRESSION* shall be greater.

Form 4555 - Savings Journal

19 ___	SAVINGS JOURNAL				19 ___
ACCOUNT REGISTER					
INSTITUTION	TYPE (CD, Passbook)	INTEREST RATE	PRINCIPAL	MATURITY DATE	VALUE AT MATURITY OR AT YEAR END

THREE - YEAR SUMMARY

YEAR	Total Deposited	Total Withdrawn	Net Saved	Net Increase/Decrease
3 YRS AGO: 19___				
2 YRS AGO: 19___				
LAST YEAR: 19___				
TOTAL				

MONTHLY JOURNAL

Line		JAN	FEB	MAR	APR	MAY	JUN
1	Total saved monthly - previous year						
2	Projected Monthly Goal - Current year						
3	Projected Increase over previous year (line 1 - 2)						
4	Actual monthly savings - Current year						
5	Actual increase over previous year (line 1 - 4)						
Line		JUL	AUG	SEP	OCT	NOV	DEC
1	Total saved monthly - previous year						
2	Projected Monthly Goal - Current year						
3	Projected increase over previous year (line 1 - 2)						
4	Actual monthly savings - Current year						
5	Actual increase over previous year (line 1 - 4)						

ANNUAL SUMMARY

Projected Annual Savings (Total Line 2) >		Actual Annual Savings (Total line 4) >	
		Total Life's Savings at start of current year >	
		TOTAL SAVINGS - YEAR END	

Copyright (c) 1991, MMI 4555

(An illustration of Form 4555 by MMI—an example of a savings journal.)

IMAGINE THE VICTORIES

Pause for a moment, and reflect on the internal power this technique harnesses. Visualize yourself, having stretched to a new record, then unconditionally requiring yourself to shatter *that* record in the *succeeding* cycle. Never allowing yourself to rest on "good enough," you will accept only "better than ever before." Just think what that will do to your reservoir of money. Then think of what that will do to your reservoir of personal strength! This process, if turned into a perpetual habit, will vault you to absolutely stunning levels of accomplishment in a few short years.

My grandfather told me, "The best compensation for doing something hard is that it increases your ability to do something harder."

I hope you will, in fact, pause for a moment and visualize yourself implementing this technique. You will begin to sense its potential on many levels. Ponder and meditate on the ways you could apply this idea, and you will feel something kindle inside you. You will feel an excitement about reaching higher achievements than ever before.

As good as it may feel to you now, you do not yet know the half of it. You will not *really* have any idea of the full efficacy of what I am teaching you until you have actually applied it for 16 to 18 months. It will take you 12 months to complete your first savings cycle. That will be a notable beginning, but it is only small portent of things to come. Once you have established your first baseline, the combination of definitive self-comparison, the spirit of internal competition, and the power of keeping every promise can finally be brought to bear.

You will save like you have never saved before. Throughout that second cycle, you will have a greater resistance against temptation and rationalization. The momentum builds and so does your own inner strength. By the third year, the transformation in your self-mastery will be nothing short of phenomenal. The technique works, and it is potent. It derives power from the triad cited earlier—the power of cycles, the power of internal competition, and the power of small means.

Some people never learn how to properly channel their inner drives and powers. They spend all of their time dissipating their energy, trying to surpass their neighbor. They would make infinitely greater progress if they would *internalize the energy* and work at surpassing their own records, year after year.

OFFER A REWARD

There is one more element in human nature to consider: We human beings thrive on rewards. Another way to enhance your Savings Plan is to weave a reward system into it. As a rule, we are able to exert discipline and forego immediate indulgences if we can see that delayed gratification will pay off in the long run.

Here is a recommendation: Set a savings goal for the next three months—something lofty but not too strenuous. Then devise an appropriate reward for yourself which you will bestow when you achieve it—a weekend getaway or dinner at your favorite restaurant. Small rewards add an element of fun and incentive to your quest. When you have reached the first goal and rewarded yourself, up "the ante" and commit to another goal and reward.

I have set up a *series* of savings milestones and rewards. Like rungs on a ladder, they inspire me to press ahead steadfastly, not splurge when the urge hits, and, in general, to stay true to my mind set of accumulating money. At each progressive milestone, the reward is greater; and I always make these rewards exciting enough to supply myself with genuine incentive.

One clarification: Do not take money from your savings account to fund the reward. Instead, work it into your budget. Never consider your savings, or the earnings on your savings, as spendable until you have achieved the overall objectives of your Master Plan.

In summary:

CHALLENGE yourself.

MEASURE yourself.

SURPASS yourself.

REWARD yourself.

I challenge you to harness the power of this lofty form of competition—the competition with self. It will prove to be the most potent expression of the competitive drives within you. The benefits you will derive are superb.

CHAPTER 15

Own A Debt Elimination Plan

The third step in the Master Plan is Debt Elimination. The master of money owns a debt elimination plan.

There is no question about it, the most debilitating disease of our society is the plague of personal debt. It is the single biggest antagonist to financial freedom and monetary peace of mind. Yet, for many it has become a way of life. For most Americans, debt is as constant as the sunrise. It would seem, like oxygen, it was a requisite for life itself. Most will go to their graves never knowing the serenity that comes from being completely, totally, entirely out of debt. Meanwhile, modest to momentous fortunes in interest payments and finance charges pass through their hands as they funnel their cash to one creditor after another, year after year.

One of the simplest monetary truths of the ages never quite sinks in: "Interest. Them's that understands it, gets it. Them's that don't, pays it." INDEBTEDNESS IS BONDAGE! That is not just melodramatic rhetoric; it is the literal truth! Paying interest is a form of servitude, the most relentless form.

J. Rueben Clark, lawyer, statesman, and U.S. Diplomat stated:

> Interest never sleeps nor sickens nor dies; it never goes to the hospital; it works on Sundays and holidays; it never takes a vacation...it is never laid off work nor discharged from employment; it never works on reduced hours...it has no love, no sympathy; it is as hard and soulless as a granite cliff. Once in debt, interest is your companion every minute of the day and night; you cannot shun it or slip away from it; you cannot dismiss it; it yields neither to entreaties, demands, or orders; and whenever you get in its way or cross its course or fail to meet its demands, it crushes you.

The people who have never lived by a well-planned budget find it a very restrictive experience when they make their first attempts. What they are really feeling is the chains and limitations of debt. Their lack of discretionary dollars in the present is due to deficit spending in the past. It is difficult to live on less than one earns after a period of being out of control. Sometimes the debt service has bloated to the point that it is not even mathematically possible to maintain living expenses and pay the obligations. In such cases, a consolidation loan may be the only hope of staving off bankruptcy.

Extricating yourself from that quagmire—the quicksand of high levels of debt—takes time, but it *can be done*. The sooner you resolve to do it, the sooner you are going to know financial freedom. Do not procrastinate. Liberating yourself from debt requires more time and effort than most people realize. They do not fully comprehend that reality until they begin to actually make the attempt. Then they come to appreciate Mohandas Gandhi's astute observation: "Golden shackles are far worse than iron ones."

Those of you who have not entered into the shackles of monetary enslavement, STAY FREE. Don't be deceived by the easy come-ons for credit.

Will Rogers' insight is still as relevant today as it was in 1923:

> If Congress passed a bill that no person could borrow a cent, they would go down in history as committing the greatest bit of legislature in the world. You can't break a man that don't borrow.

Those who failed to heed his wisdom in the '20s paid dearly in the '30s.

'TIS FAR EASIER TO BORROW THAN REPAY

I am not saying, "Never borrow—under any circumstances," but very close to it. There are some times and purposes when entering into debt may be justified. Getting a college education or purchasing a home can be justifiable objectives for some debt accrual. However, even for worthy objectives, enter into financial commitments cautiously, prudently and modestly.

I have seen many young people stifle their destinies by over-mortgaging the future through excessive borrowing during their school years. With just a modicum of sacrifice they could have substantially reduced their debts. Their future would have been brighter, and their prosperity would have come sooner and been more substantial in the long run. Many people accrue so much debt in their college years they are playing catch up the rest of their lives.

The same principle holds true with home mortgages. Do *not* stretch yourself to the maximum and "grow into your house and payments." Paying interest does not build equity! Run (don't walk) from the financial advisors who tell you large mortgages are a good idea because Uncle Sam will allow you to write-off a chunk of the interest. The flimsiness of that logic has already been demonstrated (Fallacy No. 4).

Home Equity Loans are also to be avoided at all costs. They are a virus. They may lie dormant for a few years but sooner or later they will manifest their ills.

This very nasty condition will result in much sorrow and misery. The time is not far distant when many will lose much, because of the subtle ease of frittering away their equity through the currently popular Home Equity Loan propositions. You can bank on it. (Pun intended.)

Even if Uncle Sam would let you write every last cent of interest off your taxes, you are still not building equity, or gaining ground on ownership, or building an estate, or adding to your net worth, by paying large sums of interest.

HOW MUCH IS TOO MUCH?

This advice, I realize, may be arriving "post disastrum" (fictitious colloquial Latin is my sub-specialty). If you *know* you are in deep water in terms of debt, you must embark on an immediate and undeviating course of debt elimination or deal with bankruptcy. Both of these options will be discussed later in this chapter. If you are not sure about your debt situation—not certain how much debt is too much—here are some rules of thumb upon which to make a judgment.

Over the years, the lenders have employed a simple guideline for evaluating risk levels. They calculate a "debt-to-income ratio" for the hopeful borrower. (This is why borrowers must submit those revealing confession sheets filled with personal disclosures known as financial statements.) The debt-to-income ratio serves as a metric to measure the borrower's financial buoyancy. This ratio is easily calculated.

To arrive at your own, follow these simple steps:

1. MAKE A LIST OF ALL YOUR FIXED DEBT PAYMENTS.

You may wish to use something like the Debt Schedule Form—Form 4530. (An illustration of this form is shown on the next page.) The form is designed to jog your thinking, to help you recall and list *all* debts.

Please note that you do *not* include obligatory expenditures such as food and utilities. They are monthly recurring necessities, but they are not *contractually* mandated debts. (That's one of the points in all of this. You have monthly necessities which are essential, and you must spend money for those. If, in addition to that, you have added a good deal of debt obligation, you are caught in the squeeze between necessities and debts.) Do not fudge. List *all* debts.

Most home mortgage payments include not only principal and interest, but taxes and insurance as well. If your mortgage payment does *not* include both of those figures, add those amounts to your mortgage payment amount. They are obligated mortgage-related expenses and must be considered part of the debt picture. If you are renting, do not include this amount on the list. We deal with that issue shortly.

2. DETERMINE YOUR TOTAL MONTHLY DEBT PAYMENT.

Add the minimum monthly payments of all of the debts on your list. This is your TOTAL MONTHLY DEBT PAYMENT. Now divide this amount—your Monthly Debt Payment—by your monthly net (after taxes) income. The answer you derive is a percentage. It is your DEBT-TO-INCOME RATIO.

According to the lending institution guidelines, if you are seeking a mortgage, your monthly payment (PITI—principal, interest, taxes and insurance) should not exceed 25 percent of your monthly gross (before taxes) income.

FORM 4530 - DEBT SCHEDULE

19 ____	DEBT SCHEDULE			19 ____
(A) LONG TERM DEBTS		**(C) PRIORITY CHART**		
(Mortgages, Auto Loans, Etc.)		(List Creditors from smallest balance to largest)		
Creditor	Remaining Balance	No.	Creditor	Balance	Mo. Payment

Creditor	Remaining Balance	No.	Creditor	Balance	Mo. Payment
		1			
		2			
		3			
		4			
		5			
		6			
		7			
		8			
		9			
		10			
		11			
		12			
		13			
(B) SHORT TERM REVOLVING DEBT		14			
(Charge accounts, Credit Cards, Etc.)		15			
Creditor / Present Balance		16			
		17			
		18			
		19			
		20			
		21			
		22			
		23			
		24			
		25			
		26			
		27			
		28			
		29			
		30			

Total Monthly Debt Payment

INSTRUCTIONS: If you are not on the Debt Elimination Plan, transfer the Total Monthly Debt Payment to Column (D) on the Cash Flow Chart, Form 4525. (Since this will be a constant for the entire year, the Payment amount is entered on each line of Column (D). If you are on the Debt Elimination Plan, add 5% of your monthly take home pay to the Monthly Debt Payment and enter that sum on each line of Column (D).

Copyright (c) 1991, MMI   4530

(An illustration of Form 4530 by MMI - an example of a Debt Schedule.)

Furthermore, they have a standard ratio for *total* fixed debt as well. This varies somewhat, but most lenders start backing off when the percentage of all debts (including the mortgage payment) falls in the neighborhood of 40 percent of the monthly *net* income. Some have gone as high as 45 percent but have lived to regret it. (Seen any sinking S&L's lately?) People in that position are a poor risk, because their discretionary dollars are severely limited. They are headed for Default City.

Accordingly, if you are not presently paying on a mortgage—you are renting or have your home paid for—your debt-to-income ratio should not be over 15 percent of your net income. Compute your own ratio. If your debt-to-income ratio is above 40 percent (15 percent if you are renting), you are skating on very thin ice. Reason and prudence beg you to get back to the 25 to 30 percent level; and I am asking you to aspire to having no debt at all!

THE DEBT ELIMINATION PLAN

The following Debt Elimination Plan is tried and proven to be an effective method of lowering and eliminating the devastating drain of debt. It works in any economic climate and in any state in the Union. It is straightforward and unambiguous.

Once you have mastered the first two steps of the Master Plan—you have (1) committed yourself to the Accumulation Mind Set; and (2) mastered a monthly savings habit, paying yourself at least 10 percent per month—then you are ready to embark on the Debt Elimination Plan. It has subtle beginnings which gradually, but steadily, increase in potency with remarkable results.

Right now you have a certain amount which is obligated each month to your creditors. This is the present debt service amount you computed on Form 4530. Under the Debt Elimination Plan, this amount is going to remain unchanged throughout the debt requiting process. Following the steps I am about to outline, you will be able to pay off large chunks of debt without drastically impacting your monthly budget.

Start by subscribing to the following three rules:

(1) ACCRUE NO MORE DEBT.

NONE. From this point on, deficit spending is not an option. Be tough. Live within your income.

(2) SET A SPECIFIC DEBT ELIMINATION GOAL.

Start with your debt-to-income ratio. What would you like that ratio to be? It's up to you, obviously. You may choose any percentage between 0 and 40 percent. I recommend it be not more than 25 percent. In fact, I would like you to consider totally debt-free living, in which case your goal would be 0. Give it some thought.

You do not need to do it all at once. You may wish to set an intermediate goal. Achieve that first mark, and then reassess at that point. Weigh things carefully, and set the goal. Make yourself a promise! Write it down. Refer to it often.

(3) USE NO DEBT PAYMENT MONEY FOR ANYTHING BUT DEBT ELIMINATION UNTIL YOU HAVE REACHED YOUR GOAL.

You are going to achieve your goal using the money which is presently going to your creditors. As, one by one, you pay off those debts, money will be "freed up." Not one penny of that "freed" money must leave the debt elimination program. That money will be used to accelerate the rate of repayment on your remaining loans.

THE STEPS IN THE PLAN

We now move from the rules to the implementation:

STEP NO. 1: DETERMINE YOUR SEQUENCE OF ATTACK.

Return to Form 4530-Debt Schedule. There is a place for you to list all your debts in a random order. There is also a place to reorganize that list into a definite order. On the place designated on the form (Section C, Priority Chart), proceed to relist you debts from the smallest *balance* to the largest.

This reorganized list becomes your "order of attack." You will begin eliminating your debts one by one, focusing on the smallest debt balance first. Irrespective of interest rate, payment amount, or any other consideration, you are going to eliminate the *smallest balance first*. The purpose is to eliminate one dem and from your debt service and one worry from your mind as soc 1 as possible. It also frees up some capital (not to mention the escalating cost of an envelope and one postage stamp).

If you are in a high debt position, 33 percent or above, I suggest you accelerate the debt elimination by making a temporary modification in your savings plan. If you can avoid this modification, do so. However, if you are stretched to the hilt as it is, you will need to employ this suggestion:

Divide your monthly savings allotment in half. One half (or 5 percent of your net monthly income) will still go to savings. The other half will be used to accelerate the debt elimination.

STEP NO. 2: PAY OFF YOUR SMALLEST DEBT FIRST.

On all but the smallest debt, pay the minimum monthly amount necessary to keep the account in good standing. On the smallest, pay not only the required payment, but also the 5 percent of your net monthly income previously committed to savings (or whatever portion of that 5 percent which is needed to requite that debt; if any money "spills over" apply it to the next debt on the list). Shortly, you will have paid that debt off (hopefully the first month) and will have liberated some capital. At first, the plan will look like this:

DEBT ELIMINATION PLAN

1. Debt 1	Minimum Payment + **5%**
2. Debt 2	Minimum Payment
3. Debt 3	Minimum Payment
4. Debt 4	Minimum Payment
5. Debt 5	Minimum Payment
6. Debt 6	Minimum Payment

STEP NO. 3: ROLL ALL FREED CAPITAL ONTO THE SUCCEEDING DEBT.

When the first debt is gone, continue to use this debt service money for the purpose of eliminating debt. Leave it in the plan until you have reached your goal. With your first obligation out of the way, roll that money onto the payment of the next debt on your list (Debt 2) along with the additional 5 percent, until that debt is expunged.

Your debt picture will then look like this:

2. Debt 2	Minimum Payment + **D1 + 5%**
3. Debt 3	Minimum Payment
4. Debt 4	Minimum Payment
5. Debt 5	Minimum Payment
6. Debt 6	Minimum Payment

STEP NO. 4: CONTINUE THE PROCESS UNTIL YOU HAVE REACHED YOUR GOAL.

With the erasure of each debt, ALL the freed money is rolled onto the payment of the succeeding debt. The process continues until you have reached your debt elimination goal. Each time one debt is eliminated, the process accelerates a bit. What begins as a trickle soon becomes a stream and eventually a torrent. By this simple and reasonable technique, hefty amounts of debt can be expeditiously requited.

The plan is graphically represented as follows:

DEBT ELIMINATION PLAN

1. Debt 1	Payment + 5%
2. Debt 2	Payment
3. Debt 3	Payment
4. Debt 4	Payment
5. Debt 5	Payment
6. Debt 6	Payment

When Debt 1 is eliminated, proceed to:

2. Debt 2	Payment + D1 + 5%
3. Debt 3	Payment
4. Debt 4	Payment
5. Debt 5	Payment
6. Debt 6	Payment

When Debt 2 is eliminated, proceed to:

3. Debt 3	Payment + D1 + D2 + 5%
4. Debt 4	Payment
5. Debt 5	Payment
6. Debt 6	Payment

When Debt 3 is eliminated, proceed to:

4. Debt 4	Payment + D1 + D2 + D3 + 5%
5. Debt 5	Payment
6. Debt 6	Payment

And so on, until you have reached your goal.

ANOTHER APPLICATION OF THE SUCCESS FORMULAE

In the previous chapter I have recommended a simple success formula which brings remarkable results:

CHALLENGE yourself.

MEASURE yourself.

SURPASS yourself.

REWARD yourself.

This same formula will pay major dividends when applied to the Debt Elimination Plan as well. Predetermine a few intermediate goals, and establish an appropriate reward system commensurate to the milestone. Similar to the reward system described for the Savings Plan, this will markedly accelerate your progress.

In the case of the Debt Elimination Plan, this incentive-bonus system is even more crucial. I have observed a number of households working toward debt elimination who start well and keep things going for a time. Then (and, interestingly enough, it is often just before paying off a major debt) they lapse into a splurge mode again, and march a few paces backward. The reward system provides a way of avoiding that pitfall. Tie an exciting, appealing reward to the elimination of *each* creditor. That will get you past the "almost there" splurge syndrome.

To fund your milestone bonuses, allow yourself a little latitude with the "freed up" capital. This differs from my recommendation in regard to the Savings Plan. Here I think it is okay to take a break from the program once in a while. In fact, I recommend it—as long as you do not take such breaks too often, or make them too long.

When you have completely, totally paid off one of your major creditors, especially if this has been a rather large debt, take one month off the debt elimination quest. The month after you have paid off the debt, take all of the "extra" money you have been using to pay off debts and do something fun or exciting with it. Do something out of the ordinary; something you will remember. Make it a memory.

You may not be able to do much when you reach the first milestone or two, but that will change. As, one by one, your creditors are eliminated, the "extra" money available will increase nicely. Down the road a little, you will have a fairly tidy sum with which to reward yourself.

Plan ahead. Set your goal and reinforce the images of the reward to your mind on a frequent (daily) basis. When Susan and I were using this plan, we liked to use a vacation or get-away trip as an incentive. We set our goal to go to a certain enticing spot in the world, (commensurate with the amount of money we had to play with at that point) and we would get a few travel brochures or posters depicting the destination. By hanging those visual symbols in strategic locations around the house, we created an effective way of keeping a little fun and excitement in our debt elimination goal. Best of all, it kept us from splurging *before* we had actually reached the milestone we were seeking.

If you want to accelerate the debt elimination process, after an *above average effort and accomplishment*, give yourself two or three months "off" and really do the reward thing up tidy.

Challenge yourself to achieve one of your loftier debt retirement milestones four to six months earlier than planned. Affix a correspondingly lofty reward—one that you could afford with three months' debt elimination money. When you reach your milestone *earlier* than projected, you will have saved a pile of money, and I suggest you reward yourself with *some* of the savings.

By fixing your mind on a bigger-than-usual reward you will achieve a higher-than-projected performance. In such a case, it is more than appropriate to put the debt elimination plan "on hold" for a couple of months, and give yourself a generous reward-bonus. Hit your target, and do it early. Reward yourself, and savor it. Then dive back into the debt elimination program, looking forward with rejuvenated energy to your next milestone and reward. It is quite amazing how well this idea works.

CHALLENGE yourself.

MEASURE yourself.

SURPASS yourself.

REWARD yourself.

A WORD ABOUT BANKRUPTCY

Some people who read this book may be in such painful financial straits that it is virtually impossible to get themselves out of debt by employing this or any other reasonable method of debt elimination. For those who have never been in such a predicament, it is easy to pass judgement. To you who have been spared such anguish I say, "Count your blessings. There, but for the grace of God, go we all."

There are many fine, honest people who through no egregious malfeasance on their own part find themselves trapped in a bed of financial quicksand. If you are one of these, this is what I have to say:

We live in a great land. There is an inspired set of principles which have provided liberty and a reasonable degree of justice for all. (Things are not perfect in the USA, but they are not much better anywhere else on earth.) Within the framework of the law, there exists legal and just provisions for debt relief. True, there have been abuses, but not everyone who seeks protection under those provisions need feel like a criminal or a deadbeat. Many, due to spiritual, religious and/or moral convictions, hesitate to consider bankruptcy as an alternative to their financial plight. That is good; it is right to resist the course of last resort. However, the bankruptcy laws are enacted, in my opinion, precisely for people who have that type of moral fiber but who have no other reasonable alternative to their monetary nightmare.

Often it is difficult to even obtain the facts upon which to make the decision. People hesitate to consult an attorney when they are in deep financial distress because they know they can not afford the legal expenses. I am not trying to give anyone's services away, but there is another small ray of good news. There are attorneys who specialize in bankruptcy law. Most of them will extend themselves, free of charge, for a consultation to help you get some answers and ascertain whether this is the route for you. They will expect a fee only when you employ them to proceed with the filing of your case.

Despite all the negative lawyer jokes, the majority of these people have a heart, and those who specialize in this area of the law understand your predicament. (Obviously, verify before you make the appointment that a free consultation is the policy of the attorney you select.)

It is important to understand that there are different degrees of bankruptcy. Frequently referred to as "chapters," each has its separate provisions and limitations. Chapter 7 is full-blown bankruptcy, while Chapters 11 and 13 are "partial bankruptcies," allowing you different ways of getting back on your feet without losing all of your assets.

An attorney can help you sort through the alternatives without incurring a fee. Only you can decide what is right and what is wrong for you. It is a significant decision, and you must consider it carefully. There are serious and challenging ramifications—the blemish on your credit record, for one. As you study it out in your mind, I think you will know whether it is a morally and legally acceptable route for you or just an "easy way out."

FORECLOSURES

My philosophy regarding foreclosures is similar. Submitting to a foreclosure is not necessarily a flagrant moral transgression either. Sometimes, even for responsible people, there is no other reasonable alternative. Again, it is your conscience and you must decide. Only you can say whether it is justifiable or merely an expediency to avoid some discomfort.

The decision rests largely on whether or not you feel you can accept the consequences. On the deed or in the contract—the instrument you signed to begin the deal—your creditor agreed to accept certain remedies in the event of your failure to uphold your side of the agreement. The creditor agreed to that option. It is not necessarily unethical or morally reprehensible to let him exercise that option.

If the conditions of the foreclosure are something you can abide, and it is less damaging to your estate than to fulfill the agreement, then leave it up to your creditor. Know this, however, the law is on the creditor's side in such a case.

Responsible communication on your part can help in many cases. Most people are fairly reasonable and understanding, and sometimes things can be renegotiated. The point here is to seek out all your options before you finalize a decision. Enduring a foreclosure also has its consequences. It will blemish your credit rating almost as severely as a bankruptcy. In fact, in some cases it is considered worse.

ABOUT CREDIT RATINGS

The foregoing leads us to a discussion of credit records and credit ratings. The first thing to understand is that a spotless credit rating is a valuable asset—one to be achieved and preserved. If you have a strong credit rating, it increases your financial options. If your credit record is good, keep it that way.

For those of you who are debating alternatives such as foreclosure or bankruptcy, here are some thoughts. First, know this: Blemishes on your record linger. They will be there for 7 to 10 years, depending on your state's laws. That is not the end of the world, but make no mistake about it: You will live with that record, at least to some degree, for close to the next decade.

Before moving on, let us deal with the issue of Credit Repair Agencies I refer to the firms who claim to be able to clear your record. My advice: "Lock up your purse, Gladys, and head for the car." Don't get involved with them. There is nothing they can *legally* do for you which you cannot do for yourself.

If the items on your record are incorrect, you can rectify the situation by written documentation through the creditor who made the report or with the credit bureau itself. You do not need to pay a third party to accomplish that. If the information is correct, there is no legal way to expunge the blemish. The companies which claim such ability use unlawful tactics, such as substituting Social Security numbers of people who have died and various other ingenious, but felonious, ploys. Stay away from them.

REBUILDING YOUR CREDIT

When your credit rating is defaced and imperfect, all is not lost. You can get yourself back into fairly good terms with the world in about two years. Here is how:

1. Establish Unwavering Discipline In Your Life.

Until you get some self-discipline established, a poor credit rating can actually be a blessing. Easy credit has been your downfall. Having no other alternative but "pay as you go" may well be the beginning of a cure for your disease.

On the other hand, once you have overcome this weakness, you must demonstrate that by living within your means and paying every bill promptly. As you go to reestablish your credibility with the world, any flaws here will be lethal. Stay current and pay on time!

2. Own A Savings Plan.

Live the principle taught in Chapter 14. Establish a savings account and add to it faithfully each month. That record in itself is something you can use to demonstrate to your banker that you have corrected your course. It is also a means to accomplish something even stronger, a passbook loan.

3. Obtain A Savings Passbook Loan and Repay It.

Once you have accumulated a decent sum in your savings account you can obtain a loan, using that money as collateral. This is called a "Passbook Loan." Suppose, for example, you have $1500 in your account. You could borrow $750 with little or no questions asked. You would be giving your passbook to the bank in exchange for the loan.

Until the loan is repaid, you would have no access to any of the money in your savings account. The bank would be willing to make the loan despite your past record, because there is absolutely no risk involved. If you fail to repay the loan, they will take the money out of your savings account.

Terms and conditions for such loans vary, so shop around. If you are climbing out of a bad credit situation, ascertain this information before you decide where to open your savings account. You must get your passbook loan from the same bank where you have your savings.

Obtain the loan and then make your payments flawlessly. Make sure each payment arrives a day or two ahead of the deadline and continue this practice for 6 to 12 months. You have to allow enough time for this to show up on your credit record.

As you go searching for terms and conditions, before you

choose your bank, make sure the bank reports regularly to a credit agency. This is the entire reason you are going through this whole scenario. It will do you no good if it is not reported. Once you are sure your performance has been reported and now appears on your credit report, pay off the rest of the loan early.

Then repeat this process with another bank. If you can afford to do so, you might want to be applying this procedure in two different banks, simultaneously. Don't strap yourself, obviously. Use your head, but the more entities which are reporting your good performance, the better.

4. Obtain A Credit Card.

In the very same way you obtained your passbook loan and for the very same reasons, most banks will issue you a credit card. The credit limit will be a significant amount below the balance in your savings account.

Use the card for a few purchases each month. It is imperative that you do not exceed the limit and that you pay the entire balance off each and every month. A clean payment record on a major credit card is one of the fastest ways to reestablish your credit rating because it gives you a broadly based credit standing.

5. Monitor Your Credit Record.

You cannot afford another blemish on your record. From this point on it must be flawless. It is amazing how often mistakes are made on credit ratings and someone else's glitch winds up on the wrong record. The similarity in names, transposed digits on a Social Security number, or any number of other errors can occur. Keep an eye on your record. You have the legislated right to know what your record is, who has requested information from your file, and so forth. Exercise that right. Look in the yellow pages under the heading, "Credit Reporting Agencies." Call up one or two of the larger ones and get the information on how to monitor your status. Then do it, regularly. TRW Credit Data and CBI/Equitax are two of the largest systems nationwide.

Following these suggestions, you can get yourself into a fairly good credit status within two years. When you achieve it, keep it!

CHAPTER 16

Own A Money Expenditure Plan

The next step in the Master Plan puts your positive mind set and commitments to the test. You are about to make the crucial step from theory to reality.

A ROSE BY ANY OTHER NAME

Some people don't like to say dirty words. Some people don't like to hear dirty words. Some people don't like to read dirty words. BUDGET is not a dirty word. This is stated "tongue in cheek" because so many of us experience severe power outages when we hear the word, "budget."

In my seminars, I have a way of getting around this mental blockade. I announce, "Wealthy people have mastered a money expenditure plan." The audience is momentarily thrown off balance while the real meaning of the phrase "money expenditure plan" sinks in. During that interval of stupor, they write the principle down. Many actually seem quite impressed with it. It sounds sophisticated, even somewhat erudite. It isn't until they have opened their minds a bit, wondering exactly what I mean, that they discover the punch line. But, that's the key: they open their minds.

If you are one of the thousands of people who have tried a budget and have only succeeded in discovering the depths of frustration, take heart; there is hope. I understand. I have been there, too. The good news is that there is an answer. After a lot of pain and a lot of frustration, I finally discovered a few things which have made all the difference for me. The process can work for you, and it is not really that difficult when you get right down to it.

The initial step is mental. You absolutely must first accept the idea that a budget is necessary. It is not optional. There are two important reasons why. First, it is the quickest way. (Nothing will expedite the accumulation of piles of money faster.) Second, it is the only way. (Remember the premier lesson of the fallacies in Section I: People who lack self-discipline, even if they fall into a large sum of money, do not—cannot—hang on to it.) Besides, a budget does wonders for your self-esteem and confidence, as well as your pocketbook.

Mental barriers in regard to budgets are not in short supply. An array of decrepit excuses abound. Let us briefly examine the more common rationalizations about budgets.

MISCONCEPTION NO. 1: A BUDGET IS SLAVERY.

"I refuse to live on a budget because it is nothing less than slavery. It robs me of my independence, I don't want to be bound to some piece of paper. I want to be free to spend my money how I want, when I want."

REALITY: A BUDGET IS THE DOOR TO FREEDOM!

Be careful of what is labeled "freedom" and what is labeled "slavery." There are serious overtones to consider. I have never yet heard an addict who did not say he or she wanted to be free—left alone to live life as he or she pleases. Addicts always, and emphatically, demand their *freedom*. It is a tragic misuse of a sacred concept.

The hue and cry of the morally anemic is that adherence to standards is slavery. They patronize themselves with self-indulgent rhetoric about devotion to personal liberty. They like to claim that their lack of compliance is actually the manifestation of something much higher and more noble—an all-out abhorrence of slavery.

Addicts have bad habits. There are all kinds of addicts. They only differ in which bad habit they prefer. Spending without planning is a bad habit. People who do not want to be "slaves" to a rational monetary plan of their own making are really saying that they would rather be "slaves" to their excuses *and* to their debts, bills and overspending habits.

Reality is: It is not possible to achieve financial freedom until you are able to live on less than you make, separate needs from wants, vanquish your debts, and build up a pile of surplus cash. And it is not possible to do that without a clear written plan. Period.

MISCONCEPTION NO. 2: A BUDGET IS FOR LOW INCOME FUDDY-DUDDIES.

"A budget is for nerds—the unimaginative—the kind of people that do not and never will have big money. When you have good money rolling in, you can spend all you want and you still have money left over. A budget is for methodical types who can not see the big picture."

REALITY: A BUDGET IS FOR PEOPLE WITH VISION!

Financial freedom is not a state of money. In reality, it does not have all that much to do with amounts. It is, above all else, a way of living. It is dynamic, abundant life which has, at its core, clear objectives and perspectives. People who achieve financial freedom have a vision. They know where they are going and how they are getting there. They are not dependent on luck or fortune. They have rejected Prospector's Mentality. They are committed to cultivating and harvesting according to natural law.

Those who achieve financial freedom have money—lots of it. They have lots of it because they do not let passion overpower purpose. They are in control. They do not allow impulse or whim to detract or to obstruct their achievements. They make sure their long-range objectives are the governing forces in their monetary affairs. So, they control the ebb and flow of their money with the instrument we call a budget. People with vision and purpose use a budget as the conduit that ensures that the money gets to the right places for the right results. If you truly want financial freedom, you do not leave it up to chance. You develop a pathway, then you walk it.

Reality is: It is not possible to achieve financial freedom until purpose supplants passion. A budget is the key to that. It gives you the power to make monetary decisions with your head instead of your hormones.

MISCONCEPTION NO. 3: A BUDGET IS DULL. IT IS DRUDGERY IN PRINT.

"Life on a budget is boring. It's a life of no hits, no runs, no fun. There is no room for spontaneity. I may never be rich, but at least I am going to enjoy what little money I get."

REALITY: A BUDGET IS GREAT SPORT!

If you love sport and love competition, you should love the challenge of a budget. One of the reasons for the popularity of sports is that generally the results are unambiguous. In sports you keep score. The scoreboard tells plainly who wins and who loses. Feedback is instantaneous. Events in the game are immediately reflected on the scoreboard. Players have the ability to adjust and, thereby, alter the course of the game. A budget serves in some respects as a scoreboard. You can measure day by day your successes and failures. What is more, the feedback is instantaneous, giving you the ability to adjust and improve. Thus, progress is accelerated.

The truth is, it is not possible to achieve financial freedom without a standard or without receiving feedback on your performance relative to that standard. A budget defines the field of play—the standard; it functions as a scoreboard, providing immediate feedback. Most importantly, (and better than most scoreboards) its message is preventive in nature. Through a budget, many disastrous decisions can be averted before they are physically enacted on the playing field.

A BUDGET FORM IS NOT THE BUDGET

I have talked with literally hundreds of people who are attempting to achieve financial freedom without the use of a budget. When I inquire as to why, I hear universally the same response: "I've tried one and could not make it work."

Probing a bit, I usually uncover more or less the same scenario. They talk of picking up one of the stock budget books found on the stationery shelf at the corner grocery store—one that says "Monthly Budget" or "Personal Budget" on the cover. Devoting the better part of a whole hour, they proceed to dutifully respond to the various blanks with a monthly estimate which is usually just a hazarded guess of what an "average month's" expenditure in the given category might be.

That done, they total the page. If it is in line with their net monthly income, they assume they have a budget. Their only criterion for this conclusion is they are not in the red. The assumption seems to be that a budget is meant to just keep you from over-spending. Thus, they have built a road to solvency only. If things look like they will end up in the black, they are satisfied. They have a nice warm feeling in their heart, surmising that, at last, they are finally getting organized and disciplined. Their glow is short-lived.

Unfortunately, within the first couple of days, their tranquility is disrupted by the rude advent of an unexpected bill. The quarterly auto insurance premium arrives. Somehow, budgeting from the monthly perspective, they overlooked the fact that they have expenditures which come at regular intervals other than a month (like each quarter, or semi-annually, or annually). "Well," they think, "that is easy enough to fix." So they start a minor shuffling process which takes a little away from the clothing allotment and a little away from groceries and a little away from entertainment, and "presto-chango" they have pasted their little booklet back together, and they are "still within budget."

Some other unexpected bill or necessity arrives on the doorstep, and the shuffling process commences anew. This time the shuffling reaches levels that would earn admiration in a Monte Carlo casino. This time a session in self-duping is set in motion, characterized by insincere promises and outright lies saturating the pages of their trusty budget book.

Shortly thereafter, (this interval ranges anywhere from two and a half minutes to a couple of days) this fragile ruse is exposed for what it is as another unanticipated demand occurs, and, with the combined emotions of frustration and relief, they hurl their "Monthly Budget" book at the neighbor's dog and are "finished with budgets!" Now if something akin to this Chaplinesque scene has been largely your experience with budgets, cheer up. There is hope. The fact is, you have never tried the real thing.

There are three fatal flaws in the above scenario:

(1) They are budgeting in the wrong time interval.

(2) They are beginning at the wrong end of the process.

(3) They did not devote enough time to think things through.

The adage holds true. "Two wrongs do not make a right;" and neither do three.

Here's a better way:

PRINCIPLES OF BUDGETING

First Rule of Budgets: BUDGET FROM AN ANNUAL PER-
SPECTIVE.

Just as any good business, a household absolutely *must*
budget from a yearly perspective. Attempting to construct a
workable budget from a monthly perspective does not produce a
clear vision of the whole territory. It leads to frustration in short
order. Look at the year as a whole and develop an annual plan. It
may take a little more thought at the outset, but in the long run it
saves time and money.

Second Rule of Budgets: DEFINE ANNUAL OBJECTIVES
BEFORE ANYTHING ELSE.

A budget is more than a road to solvency. It is the
expressway to the checkpoints you have plotted on your map.

If you intend to achieve $50,000 in accumulated reserves
in three years, how much do you intend to save this year?
Determine a specific amount, then design your budget to achieve
that goal. The same thing applies to debt elimination.

In short, owning a money expenditure plan is *how* you own
a savings plan and a debt elimination plan.

Third Rule of Budgets: USE A COMPREHENSIVE BUDGET
GUIDE AND DON'T RUSH IT.

You cannot sit down in a half-hour and come up with a
successful budget. It takes thought, especially the first year. Take
time to gather some facts, and deliberate a bit before you start
jotting figures on a piece of paper. Your experiences gained in the
first year will teach you much, and in subsequent years the whole
process is markedly easier. You will be able to formulate an
annual budget in one-tenth the time it will take the first year.

An effective plan (annual budget) should clearly identify and provide for the following:

1. Monthly Savings Goals.

2. Monthly Debt Elimination Goals.

3. An Estimate of Major Expenditures.

These would be discretionary disbursements which you would like to make during the budget year, such as a home improvement project or automobile purchase. Usually these are one time only expenditures of amounts greater than $200.

4. An Estimate of Periodic Expenditures.

These are regularly recurring expenditures which do not fall due on a monthly basis, such as quarterly insurance premiums, or an annual back-to-school allowance or a Christmas allotment.

5. An Estimate of Monthly Expenditures.

This is the component which most people exclusively think of when the word "budget" is mentioned. I hope from the foregoing outline, you now see how inadequate and short-sighted that form by itself really is.

A comprehensive budget guide can provide valuable assistance. One such guide, "The Money Owner's Kit," comes complete with full-size, 8 1/2" x 11" forms and detailed, step-by-step instructions for creating a budget. It may be obtained by contacting Mind Masters Institute: 1-800-622-6463. An order form is provided in the back of this book.

Once you have designed a comprehensive annual budget, charting the way to the next major checkpoint on your map, all you have to do is follow it. This leads us to the final two principles of effective budgeting:

Fourth Rule of Budgets: MAKE JOINT COMMITMENTS.

You and your spouse can be stronger as a team than you can be individually. Adopting a new habit which requires discipline is not easy for anyone. The process is greatly facilitated, however, when there is the support of another person. When it comes to budgets, united couples are generally far more successful than single individuals. One partner can bolster the other in times of temptation. As described in Chapter 13, you will take a major step forward on the road to financial freedom the day you both commit firmly and unitedly to adhere to the money expenditure plan you have mutually created.

There will come times when there may very well be just cause to deviate from your established annual budget. Let that always be a unanimous and unreserved *joint* decision.

In any given partnership or marriage, one partner tends to take the lead in monetary matters. There is nothing wrong with that. But, my firm recommendation is that, from this point on, one partner *never* deviate from the plan or enter into investments without the total support and consensus of the other partner.

To whichever of you takes the lead on monetary decisions I emphatically say, "Listen to your partner!" Time and time again I have seen grievous financial disasters avoided when this rule was observed. One spouse wanted to run headlong into a venture, while the other felt significant misgivings. In 99 percent of the cases the "mixed feelings" situation has been a warning, and the couple has been spared by heeding it. The converse is also just as consistently true. I call it the "Calpurnia Principle." Julius Caesar would have lived past the Ides of March had he not disregarded the warning of Calpurnia's dream. In that vein, I have seen serious financial debacles result when one partner has stubbornly pursued a hunch contrary to the strong misgivings of the other partner.

There are exceptions to this rule, no doubt. But they are few and far between. And I personally cannot think of one in my own experience or those of my personal acquaintances.

The bottom line: Work as a team; and strengthen one another by constant communication and mutual commitment.

Fifth Rule of Budgets: BE TOUGH.

The only thing I would add is a reminder of the power of repetition when it comes to dominant thought management.

Once your budget is written—the final decisions have been reached—make at least two copies. Keep one in your desk or in a file; but, most importantly, *have a copy with you at all times.* I carry mine in my Organizer, where I also keep my checkbook. I want that governing document to directly affect how I live. To do that, I must review it frequently—not just at the end of the month.

Keep in mind that one of the major functions of your written budget is to give you constant feedback. It is your scoreboard. You are not going to win this victory if you do not refer to that budget guide constantly. Have it handy, and *use* it.

REPRISE

Throughout the book I have been alluding to the direct correlation between monetary discipline and personal power. Mastering a money expenditure plan is one of the essential keys.

CHAPTER 17

Own A Tight Ship

A time-proven truth is that a small leak can sink a great ship. Monetarily speaking, it is a wonder there are any ships floating at all these days. The rapid expansion of credit has become so accepted and commonplace that very few of us stop to assess the leakage and the incredible damage that is occurring to our ships through these very subtle ruptures in our vessels.

Here, my friend, are three ideas well worth your scrutiny. They will help you own a tight ship.

Idea #1. BEWARE THE HIGH PRICE OF INSTALLMENT BUYING.

Once again, from the wisdom of Will Rogers:

Interest: them's that understands it, gets it. Them's that don't understands it, pays it.

What Will is begging us to understand is that we pay an exorbitantly high price for installment buying. Virtually everyone from the Baby Boomers on down, however, are so used to buying things in installments that the full story is scarcely examined.

Congress has enacted "truth-in-lending" laws which require disclosure of the costs involved in an installment purchase, but even that does not seem to wake people up. They keep right on destroying their estates through this insidious practice. And the truth is: The truth-in-lending form is *ONLY PART* of the truth! Here is what I mean:

Suppose a young married couple, both age 25, has a two-year-old car and is thinking about something a little "classier"—something with a little more "image." They buy a $15,000 automobile on "easy credit terms." The dealer offers them a trade-in value of $3000 on their old car and they finance the remaining $12,000 at an interest rate of 12 percent per annum. They want to keep their monthly payments at a minimum so they finance this over a five-year term (60 payments). (Of course, no one you know has ever done such a foolish thing. This is only hypothetical.)

According to the "TRUTH IN LENDING FORM," they are told that their real costs are as follows:

The Truth -In-Lending Form

Principal Financed	$12,000
Number of Payments	60
Monthly Payment Amount	$267
Total Payments (60 X $267)	$16,000

FINANCE CHARGE	$16,000 (Total Paid)
	- $12,000 (Principal)

TOTAL INTEREST..........$4,000

TOTAL PRICE OF THE CAR $15,000 + $4,000 = $19,000

What do they actually end up paying for their car? $19,016, you say? That is what the Truth in Lending Form says, but look closer. Truth in Lending is really a misnomer; the figures only tell the *obvious* costs. Let's look at the real costs.

Suppose the same young couple had kept their present car for that five-year period and, instead of paying the finance company the $16,016, they paid themselves that same amount, putting the $267 in a passbook savings account each month. Suppose also, every time they accumulated $1000 they would roll that into a Certificate of Deposit. For simplicity's sake, let us say they wound up averaging 9 percent interest, compounded monthly.

Take a guess at how much they would have had in the bank at the end of the 60 months. Not $16,016. They would have been receiving interest along the way, and through the wonder of compound interest, you will be happy to know, they would have had $20,130!

Suppose now the couple buys a new car, paying cash. Let's say they buy a car at this point which costs $16,000. Since their present car has depreciated over the last five years, suppose they get only a $500 trade-in. Therefore they must pay $15,500. Taking from their savings, they pay cash. They would now have $4630 remaining in the bank and they are age 30. If they leave the money in the bank until they retire at age 65, take a guess at the amount they would have. By then, the sum would then have grown to an astounding $94,516!

Ultimately, the new car they bought at age 25 cost them over $110,000! If they would have waited five years and paid cash they would have gotten the car and a retirement bonus of over $94,500!

The amazing thing about this example is that, other than going without the new car initially, it would not have changed their lifestyle or their budget one iota. This couple would still be paying the $267 for five years. Either way, they would be getting along without that money in their budget as they meet the rest of their needs.

On one hand they would do without the money, because it would be *gone*. They would have no savings account to dip into because they didn't accrue one. (This is the grand benefit of installment buying—NO TEMPTATION!)

On the other hand, because they would be disciplined and live life as though that savings account did not exist, although they would have a gradually burgeoning nest egg, the money would not be considered in their budget, because it would be "untouchable."

Their budgeting lifestyles would not be affected either way. No extra money would be put into the daily operating budget in either case. In the first case, it would be because they couldn't; in the second, it would be because they wouldn't.

Their occupational lifestyles would not be different either way. Neither husband nor wife would have to get up earlier, take on extra tasks, or expend more energy or effort. All they would have to do is to make sure every month that about thirty days go by. (Consult your calendar, if you think this is an extraordinarily complicated task.)

There is, however, a difference—a huge difference. Their *mental-emotional* lifestyles would differ markedly. If the couple has a burgeoning little nest egg, they would live a less stressful life. They would have a little security. They could go to bed every night with the comfort of knowing that they would be covered in the case of an unexpected emergency, and, excepting that emergency, they would have a pleasant dividend awaiting them later on in life. Psychically they would be more healthy. They would have taken a step that would free themselves from the worry, anxiety, preoccupation and distraction of hand-to-mouth existence.

To accrue this enviable benefit, all they would have had to do was to exert a little self-discipline for five years. They simply would have had to avoid installment buying for that short span in their early married life. Then they would only have had to take the gain, put it in the bank, and leave it there.

Will Rogers was not taken in by the ease of credit:

> Borrowing money on what's called `Easy Terms' is a one-way ticket to the poorhouse. If you think it ain't a sucker game, why is your banker the richest man in town? Why is your bank the biggest and finest building in your town?

It is imperative that you stop all leaks, big and small. By now, you should be paying yourself 10 percent first and feeling good about it. How about making the other 90 percent pay off a little better too? Statesman John Randolph said it well, "I have discovered the philosopher's stone, that turns everything into gold: It is, 'Pay as you go'." If you will follow his advice, you will be light years ahead.

THE VALUE OF EARNED MONEY VS. BORROWED MONEY

There is another *very* important point to be made here. It is another jagged edge on the installment trap which is usually overlooked. PEOPLE SPEND BORROWED MONEY LESS CAREFULLY THAN THEY DO EARNED MONEY.

Borrowed money is hard to value. It does not seem all that much harder or more strenuous to borrow $14,000 than it does to borrow $12,000. People tend to spend more for a car—they do less shopping, they do less bartering, they are less discriminating about options and extras, they are not as persistent in getting the salesperson down to the bottom line—when they finance a large part of it, than when they pay cash for it.

I learned this from personal experience. The first sports car I purchased was a splurge. I paid dearly for it, too. I decided to finance a large part of it, and it was so easy to rationalize. The passions were really percolating, and I made a half-hearted attempt to hammer on the salesperson and do some bargaining. (It was a pathetic attempt really.) I wound up getting about every extra there was. The difference in the monthly payments was not all that great, it didn't seem. So I bought my car.

I enjoyed the car, and eventually I did get it paid for. During the period of my installments, I came to realize some of the concepts which I have just shared with you; and I had become more wise.

A while later, I had accumulated $35,000. I had set it aside for the purpose of replacing my perky sports car, the one I had bought in installments. I had one of those prestigious sports sedans in mind, the kind a man always dreams of owning. The day I went shopping for the car, the passions were percolating once again. The test drive proved the car was everything I had been dreaming about. Then the negotiations started, and I began to realize the power of the truth: PEOPLE ARE NOT AS CAREFUL WITH BORROWED MONEY AS THEY ARE WITH EARNED.

I had worked hard to earn the $35,000. And, I had worked almost as hard to save it. That $35,000 chunk felt good in the bank, and there was a feeling of satisfaction owning that money. The more I began contemplating actually taking that whole amount and exchanging it for the sports sedan, the more I examined the whole transaction in my mind. I began to weigh things more carefully. Reason started to deal with the passions.

For a while I decided that I was definitely going to have that car, but I was not going to pay one cent more than the dealer's bottom line. I was going to get that car for a whole lot less than the $35,000, so I could keep as much of my cash as possible. So I bartered and negotiated. I was so proud of myself. I was not my usual patsy self; I was tough and unflinching. After a couple of weeks and several negotiation sessions, the dealer caved in. Shopping around, checking the guides, talking to friends in the business, and playing one dealer against the other, I finally got the car down to a great price, several thousands under the first "best offer we can make you." You would have thought the salesperson was going to drop over dead when I said, "I'm going to think about it for another 24 hours."

On the way home I made my decision. When the passion had cooled and I was more rational about it, I could see there were better uses for that $35,000. I ended up driving a hard bargain on a new sports car a step down from the first one

I gave up $20,000, kept $15,000, and felt 200 percent better about the whole situation. I WAS INFINITELY MORE

THOUGHTFUL AND FRUGAL WITH THE MONEY THAT I HAD EARNED AND SAVED. It had a value that was REAL. I was not willing to exchange that for a mere car, no matter how much I was enticed.

SILAS MARNER, I AM NOT

I am going to file a disclaimer, warranted or not. Do not think I am advocating asceticism. I am not a miser, nor do I want you to be one. I want you to really *enjoy* life; and live it to the fullest. It does not make sense as the adage attests, "to go barefoot through life, so that you can be buried in silver slippers."

On the other hand, it does not make sense to live a life of bondage and worry either. This happens when your expenditures equal or exceed your income.

B.C. Forbes, publisher, said:

> The spendthrift is never happy, never satisfied. The man who has saved nothing can seldom seize business opportunities. Many a fortune has been made by the ability to seize an opportunity when it presented itself, an opportunity that called for the prompt furnishing of a certain sum of money.

It all comes down to getting value for every dollar that you earn. Paying interest is a poor value, and so is paying more than you need to for an item. When you are spending dollars that you have saved, your perspective is sharper. You sense the real value of your money, you make better judgments, and stop *many* leaks in the hull of your ship.

Idea #2. FIND THE FORTUNE HIDDEN IN YOUR HOME MORTGAGE.

One of the largest leaks in your income is the interest you are paying on your home mortgage. Here is an incredibly simple way to amass a sizeable hunk of cash by plugging a breach in your financial ship.

ACCELERATED AMORTIZATION

A substantial savings in interest can be accrued by accelerating the payment of PRINCIPAL on simple interest loans. This will work for ANY simple interest loan with no prepayment penalty. Prepaying principal on large, long-term loans like a mortgage on a home can amount to the savings of a small fortune. You give up something in deductions on your income tax form, but you will more than make up for it in net gain in your estate.

Some mortgages have prepayment penalty clauses which vary in severity. Check the fine print in your contract. If at all possible, you want to *gradually* pre-pay your mortgage. Here is an example:

Let's say, for example, you have a 30-year $200,000 mortgage at 12 percent interest. The monthly payment is roughly $2050. By increasing the monthly payment slightly, just $150 per month, making the payment a nice round $2200, you will accrue a savings of *over $210,000!* The extra $150 goes directly to principal, thus accelerating the amortization of the loan. A full 10 years are lopped off the payment schedule! The loan is paid off in 20 years instead of 30.

$$30 \text{ years} \quad 360 \times 2050 = \$738,000$$
$$\underline{20 \text{ years} \quad 240 \times 2200 = \quad \$528,000}$$
$$\$210,000!$$

At the end of the 20 years, your obligation to the lender would be satisfied. If you then just go ahead and make *yourself* that $2200 payment for the next 10 years you will add a tidy little sum to your pocketbook. Putting $2200 per month away, and gaining a modest 8 percent per annum (compounded quarterly), would give you a handsome cash bonus of over $400,000! At the end of the 30 years, you not only own your home free and clear, but you are $400,000 richer just by a slight monthly acceleration of the payment of your principal.

The benefit of accelerating the amortization of your large, long-term loan speaks for itself. What a leak to plug! This is another great way to make the part of your budget over and above your savings plan really count.

This technique alone can make the difference between "just getting by" in a few years and really knowing the freedom and mobility that can come from a large pile of cash.

Idea #3. YOU'LL NEVER SEE SAVINGS LIKE THIS AGAIN.

You can *not* save by spending. This is not exactly quantum physics, I know, but you would be amazed how many of us become confused if I just take the "not" out of that sentence. "You can save by spending" is a myth, but every day people fall for the logic (if you want to call it that). "You can save a bundle later on by spending a little bit right now" is the more complete expression of the same misconception.

Seems like it should be simple, right. Saving is saving. Spending is spending. The ploys of so many advertisers aim directly at throwing confusion into this otherwise very simple concept.

If you sit down in front of a television for any length of time you will be exposed to dozens of commercials. You will hear and see hundreds of examples of people doing something "unspeakable"—they take a perfectly honest five-letter word (SPEND) and replace it with (call the censors, Mama) a *four*-letter word (SAVE). They have stricken the word "SPEND" from their vocabulary, banishing it to advertising outer darkness. Tell me you have not heard something like this before:

> Ladies and gentlemen, boys and girls, come to our Fourth-of-July, year-end, close-out, going out of business, inventory liquidation, new and improved, anniversary, overstocked, over night, everything-must-go SALE-A-THON! You have never seen SAVINGS like this before! Everything in the entire warehouse (I was hoping he would say planet) has been marked down. SAVE like never before! With

prices like this you cannot AFFORD to wait another minute! Get down here right away. You may never see SAVINGS like this again! Everything has got to go. The SAVINGS are going to go through the roof. If you are like me, (and I know I am), you won't want to pass up a chance to SAVE THIS MUCH! Pack up the kids, pack up the car, pack up your troubles in your old kit bag and get down here to get in on this SAVINGS extravaganza. There will be FREE hot dogs and balloons for the babies.

As I write this, I cannot keep from smiling. This is not *that* far off the real thing. I hear garbage like this every night. I was trying to exaggerate it a bit. I could hardly do it. It is already bloated to the hilt.

These hucksters use every word in the book, but you will *never* hear the word *SPEND*. It is always *SAVE*. No wonder there is confusion. Do not be deceived; spending is spending. Saving is saving.

"Why do we fall for that?" you ask. Simple, we would like to believe it could be done—that we could save while we spend. Think for a minute. Most people only save money so they can get enough of it to really do some damage when they spend. What then would be more wonderful than to be able to do both, simultaneously? They could continue to spend so that more money (that which they just saved by just having spent) would somehow roll in. This, magically, would allow them to spend again, producing a new chunk of fresh savings which could then be spent. (Get another shopping cart, Mildred.) Like the perpetual motion machine (which is also fictitious) they could just go on spending forever.

"TV GUIDE" WON'T ADMIT IT

If you are one of the many "spendaholics" in this nation, and it is estimated that the numbers reach into the millions, let me pass on a suggestion. Cut down on your television viewing.

What does TV have to do with spending? When you take a step back and face reality, there is one truth about TV that comes through distinctly. It is camouflaged but barely so. TV is not an education medium. (It could be, but it is not.) TV is not an entertainment medium. It is not a relaxation medium. You may *think* you are relaxing or you are being entertained, but when it gets right down to it, YOU ARE BEING SOLD. TV IS AN ADVERTISING MEDIUM. And I am not just talking about the commercials.

Try it. See for yourself. Cut the TV viewing to four or five hours per week (not per day, but per week) and you will notice many beneficial effects. There will be less tension in your home, less bickering from your children, and a host of other benefits, including much less impetus to go out and spend money.

PLUGGING LEAKS PAYS

Don't stand idly by, staring at the horizon and dreaming while your financial ship sinks beneath you. Instead, tune in to the truths of owning a tight ship. Identify and plug the leaks that threaten your financial stability. Replace the dreaming with these sureties so aptly stated by professor and college president, Francis Wayland:

> Wealth is not acquired, as many persons suppose, by fortunate speculations and splendid enterprises, but the daily practice of industry, frugality and economy. He who relies upon these means will rarely be found destitute, and he who relies upon any other, will generally become bankrupt.

CHAPTER 18

Own Only The Essentials

Adam Smith, a respected economic authority of the 18th century, wrote a notable text on financial issues titled, *The Wealth of Nations*. It is a book which still has merit today. In that admirable tome he states:

> The real price of everything, what everything really costs to the man who wants to acquire it, is the toil and trouble of acquiring it.

With all due respect, Adam Smith was wrong! He came up short in his analysis. Far short. Acquiring is merely the prologue. It is an insidious initiation, barely a snowflake in a Himalayan avalanche, of what is to come.

COUNT *ALL* COSTS

Possessions exact far greater expenditures from owners than the paltry toil and trouble of mere acquirement. Once you have obtained something, you have assumed responsibility. As a proud owner, you are now responsible for care, maintenance and upkeep. You must protect and preserve your treasure, otherwise all the effort expended to acquire it in the first place is for naught.

Acquiring something is only the wedding. Keeping and maintaining it is the marriage. And few live happily ever after.

You see owners wherever you go. They are the ones with their sleeves rolled up, perspiration pouring off their brows, straining to repair, refurbish, or restore some mute, inanimate and ungrateful object. They are the ones covered with paint, grease, or some other unspeakable goo. They are the ones shelling out cash to preserve what they shelled out cash to acquire.

It is sometimes difficult to actually define who owns who. The owner seems to be the one whose freedom and mobility has been diminished. It is the owner who devotes time before work, after work, holidays, days off, vacations, and retirement tending the possessions. It is the possessor who's huffing and puffing, vainly trying to forestall the ravages of gradual disintegration. The possession makes no commotion. It just politely goes ahead and rusts.

Possessions don't fret; possessors do. Owners are the ones who must superintend, the ones who must pay taxes on things, varnish things, lubricate *things*, sand and scrape, caulk and putty, prime and paint and seal things. They are the ones replacing filters, changing oil, pouring over incomprehensible service manuals— winterizing, summerizing, patronizing and (at regularly specified intervals) replacing one or more of the component parts on and of...*THINGS!*

Hear it, o ye ends of the earth: ALL OWNERSHIP IS A FORM OF BONDAGE.

I know you may think me extreme, but consider my point carefully. I might not be as loony as you think. Most of us are spending our lives and creative genius taking care of "stuff." It is an absolute tragedy and, like a land war in Asia, it is a no-win situation. Owners are futilely trying to reverse the course of the irreversible.

I now present one of the grand principles of the cosmos. Only two words long, its implications are enormous: STUFF BREAKS.

Write it down. Commit it to memory. Govern your life accordingly. Think before you go acquiring all that stuff. Take a look around; everywhere you go, you see things falling apart. They are in an irrevocable process of decay, disorganization and disintegration.

This truth is not lost on the mind of billionaire, H. Ross Perot. He stated to the students of Harvard Business School:

> Just remember, if you make a lot of money, if you go out and buy a lot of stuff—it's gonna break. You got your biggest, fanciest mansion in the world. It has air conditioning. It's got a pool. Just think of all of the pumps that are going to go out. Or go to a yacht basin any place in the world. Nobody is smiling, and I'll tell you why: Something broke that morning. The generator's out; the microwave oven doesn't work; the captain is gay; the cook's quit. Things just don't mean happiness.

The point is clear: Owners are not as deliriously happy as non-owners think they are. They are walking around, muttering obscenities, with burdens of maintenance on their backs.

Ownership means responsibility. And, since that responsibility is for something which is going irreversibly downhill, it is best to keep ownership to a modest level.

OWN THE ESSENTIALS; RENT THE ACCESSORIES

I am not saying that you should not own *anything*. I am not saying that you should not own your home nor a car or two, nor some furniture or clothing. On the contrary, I am a vociferous advocate of home ownership. Very definitely: OWN YOUR HOME! Go all the way. Don't just be paying on it. Own it!

Despite what tax advisors and financial planners will say, *requite your mortgage*! And whatever you do, do not *add* to your debt. Run, do not walk, RUN from home equity loans. They will prove a blight and a plague on your household in the long run.

SITCOMS

Get yourself into a nice comfortable home and get it paid for as soon as you can. And don't go on an ego trip here either.

There are too many SITCOMs out there which are not very funny. (You know what SITCOMs are don't you? Single Income Two Children Outrageous Mortgages.) They are not at all humorous.

There is a lot more to life than making an outrageous mortgage payment for 30 years. Your home should be your castle, not your dungeon.

The tendency is to measure one's worth in the world by the size of one's house. That is really preposterous logic. Yet family after family stretches itself to the utter limits, endeavoring to pay for the largest edifice possible in which to abide. It would seem that the goal of every American family is to have a house which is sooo big that every member of the family, armed with vacuum cleaner and dust cloth, could not cover the premises, if they started at 5 a.m. Monday morning and, never stopping for breaks, meals, or sleep, vacuumed their way over the expanse until late Saturday night at which time they all collapse in physical exhaustion somewhere between the kitchen and the 12-car garage.

Ownership to a point is wonderful. I believe that ownership of private property is an essential component of free enterprise and prosperity. Just remember, ownership comes with a continuous price tag. So do not get carried away. Keep your balance and your perspective. Own what you *NEED*. Own some things that you *WANT*. BUT COUNT *ALL* THE COSTS.

No matter how plush, a prison is a prison. I know dozens of families who are in bondage to a huge house with its huge monthly payment and huge utility bills and its huge property taxes and its huge insurance costs and its gargantuan demands for upkeep and maintenance.

Own your home, my friend; don't let it own you.

CHEAPER TO OWN THAN RENT?

Count costs, especially when it comes to toys, recreational equipment and recreational properties.

I love to go to Lake Powell, that picturesque and unrepeated marvel on the border of Utah and Arizona. We love to go as a family for an entire week on a houseboat. Susan and I take all of the children from the teenagers to the toddlers. There is something for everyone at Lake Powell. Swimming, fishing, water skiing, mud wrestling—whatever.

It is a carefree place for me. Parenting is easy there. I do not have to worry about every move my posterity makes. I can turn the children loose on the beach and they cannot fracture or destroy anything costly or expensive. My liability to property damage is minimal. I do not have to be constantly saying, "Don't touch that!" or "Stop that;" or "Be careful, you might break...;" or "Watch out, you are going to...;" and, so forth. I do not have to be on the edge of my chair, trying to avert disasters by small unskilled hands.

Consequently, I relax. It is like no other place in the world. My little ones can just roam and explore. They cannot sunder that sandstone or break the lake. They cannot even stain or soil it. It is about as sandy as it is ever going to get. All we have to do is pick up and carry off the litter, (and, in that category, we try to go the extra mile).

I can enjoy my kids without verbal corrections, scoldings and warnings spewing endlessly forth from my mouth. I sleep;

they play. They sleep; we play together. We get sunburned, and sandy, and we build fabulous memories and bonds of love. I can do that because I am not preoccupied with *property* and *things*.

I've seen parents turn into boorish nervous wrecks because they just bought a brand new, luxuriously appointed, cruiser with every conceivable amenity. You know, the ones with the customized paint jobs and perfectly lacquered finishes. Those lovely boats, so fondly cherished on the show room floor, are a source of great pain and anxiety on the lake. They actually become the source of tension and conflict in the family. The parents lose sight of their primary objective, the purpose for the family vacation in the first place. Losing perspective, they resent every movement their children make: "Don't do that, you'll scratch the paint." "Stop that, you'll tear the upholstery." "Watch where you are putting your punch, you'll stain the carpet..." ad infinitum (and ad nauseam).

IT'S MR. WEBB'S BOAT (PROBLEM)

So, here is what I do: When I want to go to Lake Powell and spend a week with the family on a houseboat, I pick up the phone, call Mr. Del Webb's company, and make a reservation. I mail a small deposit to him and write a date on my calendar. I do not have to worry about tune-ups or whether the battery is charged or any of that rot. I just have to decide what to eat and how much sun block to carry.

When I arrive at Lake Powell, the friendly folks at the marina provide me with a clean, decently operating houseboat which is gassed and ready for loading. I did not have to drag it behind my car and pray it stays there until I get to the lake. (I have a friend who, while supposedly pulling his boat to the lake, looked out his left window to witness his boat passing him on the highway.) My way is less exciting. I just have to steer the car I am riding in. I do not have to worry about the boat along the way, or even launch it when I get there.

I then spend one week enjoying the sights and experiences of Lake Powell with my wife and children and have minimal concerns about the wear and tear on Mr. Del Webb's houseboat. We are responsible, clean people, and my children are, overall, well-mannered. We do not destroy the rented property, but even if we did, my worries and financial responsibility would not be overwhelming.

When our holiday comes to a close, we gather up what is left of our belongings, pay the folks $2000, and get in our car and drive home to Phoenix. I do not have to vacuum the carpets, wash the boat, wax it or even park it. I just have to leave it in the water, more or less by the dock there. If there are a few extra scratches in the paint, I don't fret, and Mr. Webb has not yet called to harass me about the condition of his boat.

Furthermore, from that point on, all of the joys of ownership are Mr. Webb's to savor for the rest of the year. If that night an unexpected typhoon brews up and sinks that nice boat into the very bottom of the lake, it barely skims my mind. I read about it in "USA Today," comment to Susan, "Did you see where all of Mr. Webb's houseboats sank into the very bottom of Lake Powell yesterday?", and heave a sigh about how unpredictable the world is, and then find a nice place for my next nap.

AND, IT'S NICE TO CHOOSE

When things go well with my scheduling, I am able to get a few weeks each year for extended family time. I look forward to those week-long experiences. They are cherished times. I love spending some of them, as I said, at Lake Powell; but what I *also* love is to *not* spend some of them at Lake Powell and take off for Disneyland instead. I also love to just stay home with the family and support my children in their various hobbies and activities. I love Rachel's gymnastics reviews and Timothy's ball games and Matthew's trumpet recitals. Above all, I love being FREE—free to do what feels fun, right and most desirable at the time.

I don't want to feel obligated or pressured by some toy or property that I *bought*! People who spend a large hunk of change on a boat or a cabin, sense pressure to spend ample time using those toys. The expenditure haunts them a little. "We've got all that money tied up in that houseboat. We'd better get up there and use it more often." So they press a little, and go there when they would really rather stay home or go somewhere else. I do not want my decisions about how to spend my *TIME* to be overly influenced by how I spent my *MONEY*. I want my *free* time to be *free* time.

Money should not be the governing force in decisions, especially when it comes to family relationships. It does not make sense financially, psychically, or emotionally. Yet people fall into this trap every day.

A houseboat these days is not a small ticket item (in case you haven't noticed). What does one pay for a house boat these days? If you are talking about sleeping and handling a family as large as mine, you are not talking under $100,000. If I really get into the ego trip, it would not be hard to spend $150,000 or more. I am not talking about a canoe here; I'm talking about the Hilton on water.

For the sake of example, let us say that *you* decide to buy a $125,000 houseboat. That is just the sticker price. Let us say that you, like most people, have to finance a major chunk of it. That adds finance charges and interest costs to your recreational tab. Next comes sales tax and licensing. (Such expenses also have the nasty tendency of rolling around annually thereafter, only this time they are called property tax and re-licensure.) These costs are followed with insurance expenditures. Then comes the question of docking or storage. (You don't just let the air out of a 40-foot houseboat and put it in your pocket. And you certainly would not want vandals to mangle your treasure.)

All of this is just a foreshadowing of what is to come. The great law of the universe, STUFF BREAKS, now comes into effect. Your gorgeous boat begins a gradual, but unmistakable, (and irreversible) voyage to rust, dilapidation and disintegration. Since you are the proud *owner* of all that, "all that" is now your responsibility; and your time, your strength and your pocketbook are the only weapons you have to counter that.

You soon find that this arsenal can only slow the process down. It cannot halt it. The disintegration happens no matter what. All you can do by throwing copious amounts of money, time and sweat at it, is SLOW IT DOWN.

If you add the purchase price and all of the aforementioned insults to your estate and wallet, the cost of your three weeks per year at Lake Powell reach incredibly staggering heights. Even when you spread that expense over a 12-year period, (the average life of a houseboat, before refurbishing is required) it is preposterous to say that it is cheaper to own than to rent.

In most cases, it is astronomically more expensive. Even if all the infinitely irritating expenses, worries and distractions were set aside, and only the principal was in consideration, the savings are notable when renting. For example, let us say you had the $125,000 cash in your hot little hand, but instead of turning it over to the boat dealer, you just rolled it into a nice CD which would pay you an annual interest of about 7.75 percent (which it would as of this writing). Your annual income on the Certificate of Deposit would be just under $9700. If each week's rental at Lake Powell cost $2500, (which is more than what it really costs right now) you could get all three weeks of vacation for $7500. Just the interest on your principal would more than cover that. In fact, you come out $2200 ahead right there, and you still have your principal working to pay for your three weeks' vacations next year; plus, you would make another $2200 during the year (plus interest on that). In 12 years, your boat would be depreciated to salvage value practically, if you own it. You'd have an old scow worth a pittance on your hands, and a file cabinet full of receipts. If you do not own it—merely rent it when you want, you would have $155,000 and no ulcers.

TO OWN MORE: OWN LESS

The essential point here ought not to be missed. The issue is not how much one can *SAVE OR MAKE* by owning less, but what one can *DO* by owning less. Own only the essentials, and you will own more *life*.

CHAPTER 19

Own Stable Investment

When it comes to money or earthly assets, nothing is *perfectly* safe. No matter what your do—no matter where you put your money—there still exists the possibility of losing it. Banks, savings and loans, and credit unions have failed and people have lost cash. Insurance companies have failed and people have lost money. Retirement funds have been embezzled or so mismanaged that innocent people have lost their retirement. Stocks have become worthless. Bonds have defaulted. Gold, silver and diamonds have been lost, stolen or never received. Cattle can die, apartments can burn down (I've wished some of mine *would*), governments and companies can fail, go bankrupt or be taken over. Even cash can be stolen, lost or beamed to other galaxies by aliens. (Well, it said so in the "Enquirer.") Bottom line: In the very absolute sense of the word, *nothing is absolutely safe*.

Accepting that as a given, the question still remains, "What do I do with my accumulating savings?"

There is no one perfect investment. The antics of inflation affect markedly the appeal of any given investment at any given time. When the rate of inflation is increasing, tangible assets are advantageous. When the rate of inflation is stable or declining, cash and cash equivalents are better. People who "play the game" flop back and forth with the oscillating swings of the economic pendulum. We are not going to play the game. Instead, we will adopt a less hectic strategy—one which creates strength, balance and growth—no matter what inflation may do.

Our approach, in the long term, will be abundantly successful and far less thought-consuming. (You are not financially *free* if you are constantly shifting and monitoring your investments no matter how much money you have.) Those who spend their life fretting about the timing of their investments, settle for pottage. Where you invest is ultimately more important than when. And what you do with your time while the money is working matters even more.

The best piece of advice for successful investing is to first get strong and unencumbered. *That* should be your first investment. Every worthy objective in your life, including successful investing, will be enhanced by consolidated financial strength. Most people get greedy, launch into speculative investing too early, get strung-out and cannot sustain the load.

Your most profitable initial investment is the combination of *debt elimination, home ownership and a healthy, sizeable savings reservoir.* Once you have achieved that goal—are living on less than you make, own your home, owe no one a cent, and have accumulated in the neighborhood of $100,000—you cannot have a bad day. (From that point on, getting to full financial freedom is a virtual cinch.)

REACHING FOR CHECKPOINT II

In essence I am saying, "Stick to the Map." Focusing on the checkpoints (Chapter 12) will serve you better than reacting to the gyrations of the economy. Once the basic plans are working

(Checkpoint I), direct your accumulations toward the two main objectives of Checkpoint II:

1. Elimination of all debts but your home mortgage.

2. Accumulation of $50,000 in liquid savings.

Work on both objectives simultaneously. If one is achieved before the other, devote all efforts to the other, until both are achieved.

Throughout the journey to this checkpoint, take a simple, conservative approach to your accumulation plan. Open a passbook savings account in a good solid bank—one that is federally insured by the FDIC (Federal Deposit Insurance Corporation). Avoid savings and loans, credit unions and banks which are privately insured. Make sure. (A discussion of what constitutes "a good solid bank" is provided in Appendix B-"How Safe is Your Bank.")

Use the passbook account as a "temporary holding bin" for funds accruing from your monthly savings. When you accumulate $1000 over the minimum balance (most banks require a modest minimum of $100 or $200), withdraw that "extra" $1000 and put the money in a Certificate of Deposit (CD) or a Money Market Mutual Fund.

CERTIFICATES OF DEPOSIT

A CD is a contract between you and the bank. You agree to deposit an amount of money and not touch it for a fixed period of time. For this "guarantee" the bank agrees to pay you a higher interest rate than you would receive in a passbook account. This is an incentive to you to leave the money untouched for the fixed period of time. You give up a little flexibility in exchange for a better return on your money.

It is, in actuality, possible to withdraw the money, but there is a marked disadvantage. In the contract, you agree to suffer a "substantial penalty for early withdrawal." (Bernardo "the Hairy" comes out of the back room and punches your lights out.) The penalty generally amounts to the forfeiture of your interest. You can get your principal back at any time, but you will suffer the loss of your interest.

The longer you tie your money up with the bank, the higher the interest rate they extend. Usually, for periods longer than 12 months, the incentive is not worth the restrictions. At this stage of the game, do not invest in a CD for longer than 12 months. If interest rates are reasonably high (in CD terms, that is over 8 percent), lock in for 12 months. If interest rates are low (less than 8 percent), lock in for six months.

Each time you accrue $1000 in your passbook account, repeat this process. Each time one of your CDs matures, roll it into yet another CD. Do some consolidating as you go. For example, if you have some money to deposit and have a CD maturing, add the new savings to the principal and interest coming out of the maturing CD, and invest in a new, larger CD for six to 12 months. The larger the principal you deposit, the better the rate of return banks will extend. (Those advantages go up in increments of $5000, usually.)

Eventually you will have achieved your checkpoint goal of accruing $50,000. Ideally, you would at that point have your $50,000 dollars divided into about five CDs of approximately $10,000 each. Each of the five CDs would be in federally insured banks (if you want to be extra careful, have them in five *different* banks). Have them staggered so that their maturity dates are about two to three months apart. That way you always have a CD reaching maturity within a reasonable length of time. If an emergency should arise you have unpenalized money available. (Never use this money, except in the case of *extreme* emergencies.) As each CD reaches maturity, simply roll the principal and the accrued interest into another CD which will mature in a year from that date. Obviously, over the years your initial $50,000 principal will grow to something considerably larger.

MONEY MARKET MUTUAL FUNDS

If the CD route sounds too complicated, simply take your first $1000 and join a reputable Money Market Mutual Fund (MMMF). A MMMF is a way of obtaining a rate of return comparable to a $1,000,000 certificate of deposit. In essence, you are pooling your money with other small investors to gain the same return the "big boys" get. That is why it is called a "mutual" fund. Such funds are administered by brokerage houses. Select one of the large, established firms with national strength.

There are several advantages to money market mutual funds:

1. Higher Yields - MMMFs compound at least monthly and many of them compound *daily*. Consequently they will outperform passbook savings and will usually outperform CDs.

2. No Fees - Many MMMFs are structured so that you pay no fees (often referred to as "loads") going in or going out of the fund. With some of the funds, however, there is a fee on one end or the other.

3. Incremental Increases - Once your account is open, you can add to it any time and in any amount you choose. Even as little as $1 can be added if you wish.

4. Check-Writing Capability - When you open your MMMF, a book of checks is issued. You are able to withdraw any amount over $250 by simply writing a check on your fund.

5. Immediate Liquidity - You can withdraw your entire fund, if you choose, at any time by simply writing out a check for that amount. (Note: This can be a *disadvantage*. You can damage your overall pursuit in a moment

of weakness. In this regard the staggered CD idea offers more "protection.")

6. Safety - If you select the right type of fund, your money can be very safe. Be aware, however, that a MMMF differs from a CD in that it *is not federally insured.* There is no federal insurance entity standing beneath you with a safety net.

Several types of money market funds exist. Each puts your money in a pool which invests in a different category of short-term paper. One type will invest only in short-term *corporate* paper. Another invests only in *government* paper such as ultra-short Treasury bills. Others will invest only in *tax-free municipal* instruments. Each may have advantages or disadvantages depending on your situation. The broker will be able to answer your questions and discuss the pros and cons with you.

If you are looking for a conservative combination of benefits, safety and some impediment to impulse withdrawal, this is what I would recommend. Select a MMMF which invests in moderate-term government paper. This is a fund which deals with instruments which do not exceed five years. Such funds offer most of the advantages listed above, but have a back end load. They charge a fee at the time you withdraw your funds. This fee, however, is graduated, and if you leave your money in place for five years there is no fee at all. The rates of return are good to excellent, and there is a high degree of safety despite the fact that there is no federal insurance.

The fee schedule for withdrawal usually starts at 5 percent the first year. It declines to 4 percent the second year, 3 percent the third. After five years, the fee is deleted. For the first two or three years, this is a sizeable penalty and thus it "encourages" you to let the money grow.

I choose the funds invested in government paper, considering them to be, in essence, "federally insured." Technically they are not. Yet, in some respects they are even safer than CDs in federally insured banks. If a federally insured bank goes under, the red tape and political/legal maneuvering could go on for months. Your money is "safe" but inaccessible during that time. Putting your money in the funds which invest exclusively in government paper has precisely the same backing—the people who print all those greenbacks in the first place, the U.S. government.

TEMPTATION BUILDS

Be aware that along the way (even after you have achieved this major checkpoint on the road to financial freedom) you are going to be severely tempted to do something more flamboyant with those liquid funds. Amazing, "once-in-a-lifetime" investment opportunities are going to come out of the woodwork to test your resolve. Getting through this stage is, in most cases, the most difficult part of the entire journey. Fifty thousand dollars makes such a "nice down payment" on some very seductive "asset." Condominiums and cabins and houseboats will start beckoning, enticing you to "enjoy your money." BE *VERY* CAREFUL.

For some interesting reason, it seems when people can get past that precarious range and achieve the $100,000 and above range, the temptations subside a bit, although they never go completely away.

This will be the toughest part of the entire journey. It is during this time that *you* are growing the most—establishing the habits which are an honorarium in and of themselves. From this point on, things seem to become easier and they progress faster.

This may well be *the classic* example of Emerson's oft quoted wisdom:

> That which we persist in doing becomes easier, not that the nature of the thing has changed, but our capacity to do it has increased.

REACHING FOR CHECKPOINTS BEYOND

The achievement of Checkpoint II puts you in a consolidated, solid position to pursue the checkpoints of your choice hereafter. The nature of each subsequent checkpoint is dependent upon a host of variables. Factors such as your age, present income, number of children under the age of 18, and myriad other considerations influence the picture dramatically. No one series of checkpoints could be outlined which would be right for all people in all situations.

In general, my recommendation for your next objective would be total and complete home ownership. Pay off your mortgage.

Own your home free and clear.

However, in some instances, home ownership would clearly be the *wrong* strategy. An elderly widow owning a home worth $125,000 mortgage-free should strongly contemplate non-ownership, for example. The costs of taxes, insurance and maintenance are factors she must take into consideration. In her situation, she would be better off selling her home and investing the $125,000 in *very* conservative ways. Even if she only earned 6 percent per year on her money, she would probably be better off, all things considered, renting an apartment for $1,000 per month.

Another example when home ownership may not be the wisest move comes to mind. I know a newlywed couple in their mid-50s (his first marriage, her second). Neither own a house, but they are trying to decide whether to pool their resources and buy one or whether they should rent a home. In the mid-1980s to early 1990s—an era of relatively high mortgage rates and declining inflation rates—they should *not*, from a financial standpoint, purchase a home. Excellent homes could be rented in most areas of the country for far less than the interest on a sizeable mortgage. In addition, the major maintenance costs would also be transferred to the landlord. They would be much benefited by renting a nice home and investing the money they would be spending on insurance, excess interest, and maintenance in a money market mutual fund.

In summary, no blanket rule on home ownership holds true. Each situation is different. For the majority, the most profitable, inflation-hedged (in the long-term) and beneficial investment they will ever make is the ownership of their own home. I believe it is also one of the safest. It balances nicely the financial picture which I am recommending in this chapter, which is heavily weighted on the cash and cash equivalent side of the ledger. (Real estate tends to perform counter-cyclically to paper and cash. When cash and cash equivalents are puttering, real estate tends to prosper and vice versa.)

Complete home ownership offers intangible benefits no other investment can provide as well. A feeling of roots, security and pride of ownership bode well for peace of mind and sound sleep. If you are raising a family, those same benefits accrue to your offspring also, and there is no price tag you can put on that.

Once you have reached Checkpoint II, your next best move may well be the accelerated amortization of your mortgage. Most financial advisers would not agree, but I am not running for office so public opinion does not dissuade me much. If you own your home, own some savings and are totally out of debt, it is almost impossible to go broke. Even if you should fall into the ranks of the unemployed, you can get by quite well on very modest income levels.

Furthermore, as stated earlier, banks and brokerage houses can go broke. The stock market can crash. By contrast, paying off your mortgage is virtually a sure thing. Despite all the talk about tax advantages and better returns in the stock market, most people are better off just accelerating the amortization of their mortgage and saving the interest.

Of all earthly assets, the one to own is the sense of security and stability that comes from owning your home, lien and mortgage free.

OTHER STABLE INVESTMENTS

In addition to CDs, Money Market Mutual Funds and the ownership of your own home, there are some good insurance-related vehicles which offer dependable growth and stability. One in particular offers several advantages: Single-Premium Deferred Annuities. These provide guaranteed money down the road and have some nice tax implications as well.

Single-premium deferred annuities usually require an initial sum of $10,000 or more. "Single-premium" indicates that you do not add to this type of vehicle as you go along. It is a one-time shot. You simply take a hunk of your accumulated savings and buy a guaranteed source of income down the road. This money is invested with an insurance company. (Again, avoid the small companies like "Shifty of Newark," and deal with a large blue-chip firm.) The insurance company contractually agrees to guarantee your principal and a certain amount of gain over a fixed period. While the growth is occurring, no taxes are due. At maturity you may either elect to "annuitize" or you may take all the money in one lump sum. There are advantages and disadvantages to each route. Your situation will dictate which is the better choice for you. There are special tax advantages at retirement if you do decide to take the annuitized route.

Annuitizing means that the insurance company agrees to guarantee you a monthly income for the rest of your life. You can even elect to accept a somewhat lower monthly income and have it guaranteed for the duration of your spouse's life as well as your own. As long as either of you live, the insurance company will send you a monthly check. The amount of the check depends on the amount and period invested, naturally.

The terms and returns vary widely from insurance company to insurance company. Check them out carefully, and take your time. Single-premium deferred annuities are, in general, a good way of balancing your accumulation picture, and for that purpose, I am recommending them. Do not put all your money there, but, for 10 to 25 percent of your accumulations, they are worth considering.

MAINTAIN YOUR BALANCE

Maintain your balance. Because the world is uncertain and corruption abounds, no investment is absolutely foolproof or safe. No one investment performs optimally in all seasons and in every part of the country. The best approach is to minimize the risk through a conservative strategy, and maintain some equilibrium.

In general, I feel that a person's best investment is a loan. Not as the *borrower*, but as the **lender**. In the vehicles I have recommended, with the exception of the ownership of your home, you are *lending* your cash to reputable entities and they are *paying you interest* for the use of your money. Day in and day out, despite the playful calesthentics of inflation, that has proven to be the best side of the equation to stand on.

To diffuse the risks, do not lend all your money to the same entity or in the same way. Diversify. Furthermore, to balance the lender-owner equation, unleveraged real estate also works well. It does not hurt to own some real estate, but do not over do it. You do not want to be strapped to the responsibilities and time-consuming obligations of ownership and landlordship (my English teacher just croaked).

Strive for equilibrium—in finances and in life. Do not put all your money in one vehicle or on one side of the inflation scales. Have some CDs and spread them around, have a nice chunk of cash in money market mutual funds, own your home and maybe one or two other pieces of unmortgaged turf, and have a few neat little deferred annuities working for you.

In addition to all that, and above all, remember, remember, life is more than a pursuit of retirement and a stack of greenbacks.

CHAPTER 20

Own An Expanding Source of Income

The Abbotts are feeling great these days. Financially, they have never felt stronger. They have accumulated $35,000 in their savings account. This is the largest their reservoir has ever been. Their income is far from lavish, but they are living within their means and enjoying a respectable lifestyle. The future looks even brighter. They recently received an increase in their income and the prospects for future increases appear virtually certain. They feel solid.

The Babbotts are feeling uneasy. They are weighed down with financial concerns. They, too, live comfortably and prudently. However, their employment situation is unsettled. Their employer is cutting back drastically. There have been layoffs recently, and rumors abound suggesting more to come. The Babbotts have $135,000 in savings, but facing the specter of unemployment, they know their savings could disappear fast. They feel vulnerable.

The Abbotts feel confident and positive with $35,000 in the bank. The Babbotts can hardly sleep at night with over three times that much. Moral of the story: Reservoirs alone do not provide financial security. Wealth is relative, and financial security has more to do with trends than amounts.

Wealth is best viewed as a monetary *flow*—a complete watercourse *SYSTEM*. It is not just the river; nor just the reservoir; nor just the dam. It is the entire system, rainfall to faucet, supplying a continual flow of the indispensable fluid which sustains life.

An effective, life-sustaining river system does not exist without a sturdy dam. It supplies *control* over the resource. In financial terms, the dam is your budget and your savings plan. It is founded on the bedrock of your self-control and discipline. Eliminating your debts plugs the leaks in the dam and solidifies the system's strength. If you do all that, you will get a reservoir. But wealth goes beyond that.

When you have a well-constructed dam with little or no leakage, and a handsome reservoir filling in behind it, you are ready to go back and tend to the river. Once the control system is in place, *then* everything that follows depends on the measure of the river itself. Two things determine the flow of a river: the amount of rainfall and the size of the watershed. Increasing either one of these factors enlarges the volume of the river. In this chapter we deal with the central keys in creating a mighty flowing, monetary torrent.

RULES FOR A RIVER

Here are the three fundamental rules I recommend for creating a mighty financial river:

1. LABOR AT SOMETHING YOU LOVE.

2. STAY FOCUSED AND INVEST IN YOURSELF.

3. SOLVE OTHER PEOPLE'S PROBLEMS.

LABOR AT SOMETHING YOU LOVE

Take this quiz:

1. When you are at work do you find yourself watching the clock?

2. Do you "live" for evenings, weekends and vacations?

3. Do you pursue exciting, even dangerous hobbies?

4. If you won the lottery, would you quit your job?

5. If you knew you were going to die in two or three years, would you leave your profession or occupation?

It doesn't take an Einstein to see where this quiz is leading, but the implications are monumental, and you may not realize it. If you are giving affirmative answers to these questions, it is highly unlikely that you are ever going to have significant amounts of money. Worse than that, you are wasting your life. I know that is blunt, but it is the truth. If you are not absorbed by your life's work, it is almost impossible to create a richly abundant income stream.

Many people think the object of life is leisure and recreation. Not so. Fulfilling *work* is the elixir of life. Robert Lewis Stevenson stated:

> If a man loves the labor of his trade, apart from any questions
> of success or fame, the gods have called him.

True, we need a share of diversion and relaxation, but study after study shows that people who love their work live longer, have less disease and ailments, and make tons more money. One researcher even claims they have fewer accidents and injuries. In short, they have more life, quantitatively and qualitatively. Those who are working merely to generate money have missed the point entirely. ONE OF THE ABSOLUTE REQUISITES OF FINANCIAL FREEDOM IS TO LOVE YOUR LIFE'S WORK.

In recent decades we have given the traits of hard work and dedication a bad name and have attached a stigma to them. Labels such as "workaholic" have become epithets to be avoided at all costs. (No one wants to be an obsessed, money-grubbing mongrel, you know.) We are programmed to think that being absorbed in one's work is tantamount to declaring oneself a soulless atheist—against "motherhood, America, and a hot lunch for orphans."

We have done ourselves an injustice. To work is a privilege, the power to work is a blessing and to be deeply absorbed in a purposeful lifework is the essence of fulfillment and happiness.

It is essential that you love your lifework; it is the single biggest determinant in your income stream. People become rich by amplifying that aspect of their life, not by speculating. Too many people have that exactly backward. They want to get rich so they can quit their present job and do "something really meaningful." Those people never make it. They become impatient and usually quite frustrated with life. Keeping their 40-hour a week job for security reasons, they yearn for the weekend. They try myriad after-hours, part-time pursuits and fall for a dozen get-rich-quick schemes. Much of their life is pure drudgery, and they never settle full-time into something to which they can devote their all.

They become bored because their capacities are underutilized. Their creative genius and drive are not stimulated or challenged. The shallowness of how they are spending their life haunts them, even when they are not cognizant of what is missing. It takes some of them a long time to figure it out. Some never do.

Conversely, those who are immersed in something exciting and meaningful are fulfilled by their work and through their work. They have a zest for living that can be had in no other way. People who love what they do, seldom have to "get away from it all." They're right there doing what they love to do, enjoying the hours of their life, instead of counting them. Even going on vacation is kind of a bother, because what they really want to do is back home. And, because they love what they are doing, they do it well. They take pride in it. They take the extra pains to polish their efforts to the highest degree of proficiency and excellence.

Consequently, these people prosper. The irony of ironies is those who focus on something they love earn more than those who focus on earning. Those who focus on earning, earn. But the sledding is tough; and the flow of money is generally slow and slight. The real tragedy has nothing to do with the earnings. The real loss is that they squander their creative genius. They die with the music still inside. Their symphonies are never written or performed.

What ultimately matters is what you do with your life— what you create, not what you acquire or earn. If you can just keep that in mind, money won't usurp such a priority in your mind, and you will be happier and infinitely more fulfilled.

Successful people live to work and love their work; they do not work just to live. I see people who have risen to the top of their field—who have got it made financially—who have *more* than enough money to see themselves through for the rest of their days—but who do not, will not, retire. Why? They are not doing it *for the money*. They are doing it, because they love doing it. If they were just working for the money, they would have been long gone from the scene years ago. They are not obsessed by the money at all; they are absorbed in their work. "Why would I want to retire?" they ask. "What would I retire to?" "I love what I'm doing."

Can we not rejoice in the barely concealed zest for living in George Burns' impish quip:

> I am booked for a concert in Carnegie Hall on my one hundredth birthday. I can't die now. I'd lose too much money!

For George, it actually has not one thing to do with money. He loves life because he loves what he does.

Those who become truly successful in life almost become synonymous with their work. They do not have to stop and smell the roses; they work in a rose garden—a rose garden of their own planting and caretaking.

LOVE ADDS THE VALUE

People who love what they are doing prosper, because, without necessarily knowing it, they are adding that "something extra." That is what gives their product or service a little more value. People ultimately recognize that, and they exchange their money to get it.

All the money you will ever receive comes from other people. In a certain sense, people must give you the riches that you seek. What you are really doing is exchanging something you have, which they want, for some of their money. It also must be pointed out that people will more readily exchange their money for something which they deem to be of higher value. Give people value; they will give you their money.

People know value when they see it. Sometimes it is difficult to describe, but they sense it nonetheless. People sense value when they see that "something extra." It is usually an intangible, not even necessarily part of the product itself. It may have something to do with the "personal touch" of a salesperson, or the extra effort in prompt delivery or in handling a question or complaint. Sometimes we perceive value based on the sincerity, or complete thoroughness, or just the outright professionalism of an individual or the company as a whole.

JOHN GIVES VALUE

I own a car. Generally it is a dependable car, but once in a while it needs some help. We have been through a lot together, my car and I, so I want good work done on my car at a fair price. When it comes to repairs and maintenance, I want value.

Maybe it is paranoia, but in times past I felt ripped-off when I have had my car serviced. I had serious doubts about value. Had.

Then I met John. Now, I have one less worry in my life. John repairs cars; and he gives you value. You can feel it. This man conveys that "something extra" every time I take my car in. He is always smiling. Even when he has put in 10 hours, and you know his body is exhausted, you still see that smile.

You can tell he loves cars. You feel it when he talks about them. He bubbles over, relating stories and offering careful explanations (including sketches) about how my car is getting along and how I need to watch for this and that in the next 20,000 miles or so. Sometimes I get the feeling John likes my car more than I do.

When my car needs something repaired or replaced, no cursory, "It'll cost you $245 bucks to get this one runnin' again, Mac," will do from John. No sir. John takes me right into the operating room. He wants me to get right under the car, poke my finger straight into the "blood and guts," so I can see for myself which part is broken. All the while he is telling me about my options, whether or not a rebuilt part may do, what I can do to "get by for a while," what will be a long-term solution, and so on.

I would never *think* of taking my car to anyone else. My friends feel the same way. We only go to John, because John gives us value. We give him money in return. And the word gets around. Customers recommend their friends to John. John is getting rich. He likes that. But what he *loves* is "fixin' cars."

STAY FOCUSED AND INVEST IN YOURSELF!

Once you have found your life's work, settle in. Contemporary author, Bill Copeland said, "If you chase two rabbits, both will escape." Do not divert your concentration from your genuine source of prosperity. Stay focused. Let the wisdom of journalist

Walter Lippmann also crystalize in your mind:

> A man cannot be a good doctor and keep telephoning his broker between patients nor a good lawyer with his eye on the ticker.

I hope one of your life's goals is to become one of the very best at whatever you do. It is a worthy pursuit, for it fosters continuous improvement and growth as a person. The qualities you obtain as you stretch for excellence allow you to command an ample income. You cannot demand or justifiably expect higher "wages" from your employer or from your society unless your contribution is expanding. This world is not fair in many respects, but I believe that it is well nigh equitable on this point. Over the long haul, in the marketplace, value extended brings its just compensation.

Study your craft. The doorway to profitability and prosperity is knowledge and expertise. Your mind is what you offer the world. The greater your mental powers, the greater your value to others and to yourself. Educate yourself ceaselessly. Read. Study. Some of the best money you will ever spend will be on the educational development of your mind. In this information-intensive, global era we are entering, that is more critical than ever before. Education can no longer be viewed as an event or a stage of life that one passes through. It must be an on-going habit, an integral part of your life and lifestyle. A part of your income must always go back into furthering your earning power. Furthermore, it is also your safest investment. The sage Benjamin Franklin observed:

> If a man empties his purse into his head, no one can take it from him.

You must do all in your power to keep your mind sharp, alert, healthy (physically, emotionally, spiritually), well-fed (physically and intellectually), and disciplined.

The time and money most people spend dabbling and tinkering in the markets would return far greater rewards if they invested in their own minds and in their own fields. A conclusion drawn from a study funded in part by the National Science Foundation puts it directly:

> Your work is more likely to make you wealthy than any bet or investment you will ever make. The most profitable place to invest surplus income is in the area which produced the income in the first place...Any investment that helps detach you from work you enjoy and makes you anxious about the future better produce a million dollar profit, because it is costing you the best chance you have, by far, of making a fortune.

This is a modern confirmation of a time-proven truth. It was well-stated in the formative years of our country by Benjamin Franklin:

> I resolve to apply myself industriously to whatever business I take in hand, and not divert my mind from my business by any foolish project of growing suddenly rich; for industry and patience are the surest means to plenty.

SOLVE OTHER PEOPLE'S PROBLEMS

You have heard it said, "Wealth went to a person's head." I prefer to think that wealth does not *go* to your head; it *comes from your head*. Wealth is ultimately a product of mind. It seldom comes from physical labor. More frequently it stems from vision and creativity. Creative solutions to vexing problems are in high demand. They always have been, and always will be.

Society does not always reward its geniuses. Mozart died alone and was buried in a commoner's grave. Galileo was exiled. Columbus was mocked. Things cerebral or abstract, especially those which disrupt cherished preconceptions, are bitterly opposed and rejected.

However, society does reward, promptly and consistently, *practical* genius. Anyone with the insight to come up with an invention, service or product—something to ease the pain or labor or drudgery of life—has generally been financially rewarded. Advertisers have come to recognize that the clearer a product is aligned with the specific problem it solves, the better. Hence the success of products with names like "Easy-Off Oven Cleaner." Doesn't leave much doubt about what it does or why you might be interested in exchanging cash for it.

The simple truth is, human beings loath exertion, despise problems and abhor pain. They will avoid any one of these (or any combination thereof) with a vengeance. Whether that be good or bad is, for now, beside the point. The fact remains, anytime someone or something can reduce labor or the costs of labor, there is demand for that service. PEOPLE PAY MONEY TO HAVE THEIR PROBLEMS SOLVED. They do it gladly. Perfect strangers will elatedly compensate you for solving their predicaments or easing their pain. This is the supreme law of temporal economics.

Calm, clear minds recognize that axiom and do not fail to capitalize on it. If you want to expand your earning power, expand the vision of yourself in the role of problem solver. The grand question you must ask yourself—the query that activates the innovative juices—is, "What problems exist in my profession, my market or in my field of expertise? What problems can I help solve for other people?" Such probings trigger the creative, workable solutions that lead to demand for *your* services.

Interestingly, the reward is usually in direct proportion to the magnitude of the problem. The bigger or more widespread the problem, the bigger the opportunity to profit by being the one to solve it. The first person to find a solution and get it publicized (advertise it) generally makes a bundle.

It seems to me to be a very just equation. You help others, you profit. The greater the service, the greater the reward. Most people do not look at problems as opportunities to render service. Instead they fret and cringe, lamely wishing the problem would just go away.

Alert, composed minds are not overcome with fear or despair. They are able to behold vistas that unprepared minds are not able to discern. Howard Ruff, financial advisor and author, once said to me, "When a good person is ready, the opportunity will present itself."

"Is it presented," I queried, "or does the individual simply see and recognize a situation for the opportunity that it is?"

I believe that, just like every other aspect of life, when it comes to money, preparation precedes power. That is why, throughout this book, I have expressed concern about the mental effects of poor monetary policy. I want you to keep it simple, so that you are prepared to really *think*. When you are worried, preoccupied or stressed about your bills, your risky investments or debts, you thwart your own creative genius.

All that we have discussed in this book has been in an effort to prepare you to effectively employ these three keys. When you are laboring at something you love, investing in your mind and are focusing on seeking solutions to other people's problems in the realm of your expertise, something significant happens to you: **Your mind is capable of seeing things other people do not see. You heighten your awareness of needs and enhance the creative/innovative potential of your mind to meet those needs.**

In effect, you expand your watershed and seed the clouds. Good things inevitably flow from that. Before you know it, rain is falling. Once it starts, it pours. The rainfall runs to the riverbed. Soon, what was once hardly more than a brook becomes a robust river, which in turn becomes a mighty torrent. Before long you have an income stream you can scarcely believe, and you will wonder where all that money was hiding during your years of struggle.

You are never too old. It is never too late. Once the preparations are properly completed, the rains will come. It can flow so quickly, that almost "over night" you go from rags to riches. Wealth does not take long to arrive, *once you get your act together*. Apply faithfully the principles in this book, and, with a bit of persistence, you will get there.

LOVE, OUR GREATEST PASSION, BEGETS PERSISTENCE

Lofty achievements and genuine success come only after a trial of your commitment. The vaults of wealth do not open to you until you have proven yourself. Persistence is one of the grand keys to success, and passion is the key to persistence.

People, who are passionately absorbed in their work, succeed because they give it everything they have for as long as they have it. Most of them have a sense of calling about their work. They are on a "higher mission." Thus they can overcome pain and setback.

No career or job is perfect. There is tedium, frustration and pain in any pursuit. But the pain is not constant, and it's not even the main experience; it's just part of the experience. People who love what they do, who are immersed in it, are not stoics, and certainly not masochists; they just have that extra something which gets them through when things are tough.

There is the poignant story of the master painter who continued to paint despite the onslaught of a progressively debilitating and increasingly painful affliction of arthritis. With gnarled, pain-ridden hands he painted his masterpieces. Sometimes tears would course down his cheeks as he painted, the pain was so great. Observers asked him why he persisted in putting himself through that type of agony. His was a simple response: "Because," he said, "the beauty remains after the pain has gone away."

CHAPTER 21

Own Freedom

I have written this book because, day in and day out, I work with people. I teach them and counsel them and observe them. Mostly, that is a gratifying experience, but sometimes it is not. Sometimes I am laden with sorrows for them. So many people are suffering needlessly, squandering their time and their opportunities to make the most of their lives.

Much of the hinderance is over the issue of money. I want people to *get over* the hurdle of money, so they can sprint on down the track to more satisfying rewards. I want people to put money in its place!

Money is *not* king. We have enthroned it, and it is to our own detriment that we have done so. Money needs to be dethroned and put back into the ranks of the knights of service—an important contributor to the good of the realm, but not the king that we revere and obey. We, by the things we do, teach our children that integrity is something one only gives lip service to. Our real bottom line is cash. That is why there is a rampant and growing loss of ethical values in the world. Graft prospers because, for the masses, spending is all that counts, and you can not spend integrity.

People are not judged by the nobility of their labors, nor the service they render but on the sole basis of their earnings and possessions. Who gets more respect in our society, an elementary school teacher or a talk show host? A wife and mother is made to feel inferior because she does not bring home a paycheck which can be quantified and converted into tangible "symbols of success." Status and respect have become things an accountant determines. They are a function of a quantity of dollars. Money does not deserve all this esteem. It backfires on us at every turn of the road.

A major trouble with judging others by their money is that we start to judge ourselves by the same hollow criterion. Jesus of Nazareth pointed that out two thousand years ago. "For with what judgment ye judge, ye shall be judged: and with what measure ye mete, it shall be measured back to you," he declared. I do not think he meant that just in terms of the hereafter; I believe that also applies to the here and now.

If you judge others by the 1040 Form, you come to judge yourself by the 1040 Form. Your money and your identity become so entwined they become indistinguishable. With that fusion comes a loss of value and of values. If you are honest and hardworking, for example, but suffer a business reversal, you get depressed because your earnings decline. You consider yourself a failure. If, conversely, you cut corners—bend the rules of honesty a bit—take advantage of your neighbor, you get ahead financially. You feel prosperous and the folks next door are also impressed. You are deemed a success. See the trap?

Thus we set ourselves up for spiritual, moral and personal debacles. What we *have* becomes confused with what we *are*. Our self-image becomes a mere reflection of our portfolio. We are it; and it is us. Yet, it is a pretty sad eulogy when only the accountant can stand up and say, "Here lies Social Security Number 808-00-9999, who turned in some great looking 1040 Forms." And who more should be pitied than those who have squandered *life* in pursuit of an assortment of assets? One day they wake up and realize that all they have to show for a life is a list of stocks and properties. That is the accounting of who they are. That is why people jump out of windows when the stock market crashes. When their money is gone, they feel like *they* are too.

This disorientation leads to self-devaluation. We lessen ourselves because the compulsion to acquire assets subordinates the person to the things. Moreover, it reduces our drives, passions and creative genius to inferior levels. You do not ennoble yourself when you reduce your mental and physical powers to mechanisms of material aggrandizement. While the purse prospers, the *person* is impoverished.

Throughout the annals of human history, more people have become ensnared in this trap than any other. This misalignment is rampant today. We give money far too much respect. With this we are diminished and imprisoned. I suppose the good news is it is a prison of our own making. Since it is self-constructed, it can also be self-demolished. We are our own wardens and jailers. We can also write our own commutation of sentence. It is up to each one of us to liberate ourself from this materialistic Alcatraz.

TOTAL FREEDOM

An obese portfolio is not what we are after. What people really want, whether they cognizantly realize it or not, is *freedom*. What we must also recognize is that financial freedom is not an event, nor an amount of money. It is not a state of the pocketbook; but a state of mind.

Refresh your memory with this definition:

Free: (adj.) 1. At liberty; not bound or constrained. 2. Discharged from arrest or detention. 3. Not under obligation or necessity. 4. Independent. 5. Not affected or restricted by a given condition or circumstance. 6. Not subject to external restraint. 7. Unoccupied; available for use. 8. Unoppressed.

The message in the word "freedom" is clear. Freedom, more than anything else, is characterized by the *absence* of things—the absence of restraint or constraint—the absence of obligation and necessity.

Now picture yourself being *financially* free. Pause for a moment and visualize the implications. Sensing the weights and financial cares that you are now bearing, picture yourself entirely relieved of all of that—unburdened and unoppressed. Reread each definition, above, savoring its personal meaning to you in that context, visualizing yourself *free* in every sense of this definition.

Do you not see that freedom, even in a financial setting, is a state, not a possession? Freedom is a state of being. It is something you experience internally.

ACCUMULATION SIMPLIFIES

Money is tricky stuff. It can be used to augment our freedom. Most often we use it to diminish it. We do not intend to; it just works out that way. Money can be used to obtain holdings and possessions (which leads to a type of bondage) or it can be used to provide freedom of movement and choice. It all comes back to the critical differentiation, made at the outset of the book, between accumulation and acquirement. At first it seems like a minute distinction. It turns out to make a vast difference in the end. The by-product of simple accumulation is freedom. The by-product of acquirement is bondage. We must be careful not to exchange the greater wealth of life for something lesser. Of all the things to own, OWN FREEDOM.

Many have become restricted and oppressed by the repetition of short-sighted choices. They become so entangled in the confusion about money, they strangle. I am hoping this book will help you solve that pivotal dilemma, so your time will be better spent and freedom of choice will be restored and amplified. My message for quite some time has been, it's TIME TO LIVE! Not to exist. Not to earn. To LIVE! To BE FREE!

The key is to accumulate money. Not material possessions—money. If you gather a pile of money, it can produce more money for you. The money works to maintain you. When the pile is large enough, and your needs and wants are modest, you can virtually live without compulsory means. You can work without having to earn. But, if you acquire a pile of "assets," they siphon more money *from* you as you work to maintain them. Most people never quite get that straight in their minds. They think the only reason you get money is to convert it into things. Money can be exchanged for something far better.

Break loose from your material shackles. Be free of all the care and bother that is weighing you down. Liberate yourself from the slavery of more bills than money. Emancipate yourself from the pressure of "just making ends meet." Get yourself free of debt and obligated monthly payments; free of paying interest which saps your strength and future; free of the cares, expenses, and labors of managing and maintaining possessions and properties and "investments." Become *FREE!*—in every sense of that blessed word.

If you will halt the relentless acquisition of things and just stockpile some money for a while, eventually you will be able to come, or go, or do, or be, much more freely.

In the first place, money is a lot easier to take care of than most of the things we buy with money. Money is quite maintenance free. You do not have to oil it, paint it, or overhaul any of its parts. Money is carefree, one size fits all. Its color matches anything that you wear.

Accumulating money simplifies your life. You are less distracted. Your thinking is clearer. You focus better and your creative genius can be tapped. The ramifications of that are limitless! (A free mind is an asset worth seeking.)

I want you to be independent; not *owing* anything to any other person or entity. I do not want you to be *obligated to pay* anything—not money—not time—not effort. I want you to have no debts upon you, no liens against you, or encumbrances about you. Free! I WANT YOU TO BE FREE OF *OWING* AND *OWNING* AND *EARNING*.

FREE! SO YOU CAN GO AND BE AND DO

When you have money earning money, your burden of self-maintenance is eased. When your pile of money gets large enough, the burden becomes quite light—eventually even negligible. You are not bound to the earning treadmill. You can take a few deep breaths and look around. You might be amazed how beautiful the world is. You might become more aware of the people around you—the people you live with, the people you work with, and the people you serve or could serve. You become aware of *other* people's *needs*, because you are not so totally absorbed and obsessed with your own.

A MIND, UNOCCUPIED WITH ONE'S OWN PROBLEMS, CAN CREATE WAYS OF GIVING WHICH SOLVE OTHER PEOPLE'S PROBLEMS. Not only does this produce wealth, but it puts you on the path to the higher realms of freedom.

Such states are impossible to obtain when you are burdened with owing people or being subject to their demands. You can do more things spontaneously. At the spur of the moment you could get involved with a good cause. You could throw yourself into some worthy endeavor without having to restructure the physical universe.

I have a good friend, who, when he heard of the terrible fires in Wyoming a few years ago, decided to contribute himself to the cause. Driving to work, listening to the radio, he heard the broadcasts telling of the large scale effort to control the devastation in Yellowstone Park. On the spot he made the decision to do something. "I want to go fight the fires. I feel protecting the environment is important."

He drove in to work, took a leave of absence without pay and went to Wyoming. He told them, "I am not sure if I am going to be gone two weeks or three. I'm just going to fight fires and do whatever I can to help up there. I am not trained and I am not skilled in fire fighting, but if I can drag a hose for somebody or take a shovel and pour some dirt on part of the fire, I am going to do it. I am going to spend two or three weeks doing whatever I can to help."

My friend is happy. He has achieved a level of financial stability that allows the freedom to give himself to a good cause, spontaneously, without weeks of strategizing and planning. He is free to go where his heart wants him to be. That is the kind of freedom I want you to have—the kind of freedom that following the principles and methods outlined in this book will bring you.

FREE TO GIVE

I would like to see you less focused on what is coming in to you, so you could find the great joy and peace of focusing on what is going out of you. Too many people, either while they are pursuing money or after they get some, want to get away from other people. They insulate and isolate themselves. The more money they make, the more exclusive the neighborhood they want to live in, the more exclusive the clubs they want to join. They put up fences around their estates and hire guards and build moats. They withdraw from humanity, put up barriers and walls, and then wonder why life seems empty and unfulfilling.

There is a very basic tenet of life which says you can not give without receiving in return. The modern maxim, "What goes around, comes around," is but an up-dated version of a principle which has been known for centuries:

> Give, and it shall be given you, good measure, pressed down and shaken together, and running over, shall men give unto your bosom. For with the same measure that ye mete withal it shall be measured to you again.

When you are obligated, you can not give completely. YOU MUST BE FREE IN ORDER TO GIVE YOUR ALL. It is not possible to give something when that something is owed. You must *pay* or *repay* that which is owed. Repayment and giving are two different things. Tendering what is demanded is not really giving.

Ultimately, I would like you to be in a such a position that whatever you do is a gift. I want you to be able to give yourself to other people and good causes. I would like you to be able to give your time, your ideas, your talents, to worthy efforts of service to the people around you.

You could touch lives. You could go for a week up into the mountains and be a Scout Leader or Youth Counselor. You could get right into life—be a part of nature and of another person's life. You could get right down there in the grit of life with the little varmints. (And I am not talking about the rodents and the insects. I am talking about the boys and girls.)

THE READING GRANDFATHER

I know a gentleman who found a "pearl hidden in a field" and awoke to a new and higher perspective. He had become successful in many aspects of his life. He held the top position in his company, a large and prosperous concern. He held leadership positions on several notable committees and boards. He was an eminent person. Yet in the midst of all that, he discovered something wonderful that he had overlooked. He found how wonderful it is, in just simple, everyday human ways, to touch another person's life—to touch a heart.

He found it unexpectedly. He was in his 50s, in the third decade of high-paced corporate management and good earnings. One of his grandsons underwent an operation and was confined to a hospital bed for a few weeks. This man decided to take a couple hours off work one day to pay a visit to his grandson. The usual pressures were on him, but he told himself it would only be a couple of hours and for just this one time. He thought perhaps he would read a short book or story to his grandson, and then get back to the office. So he found his grandson, and also another little boy who shared the same room. The grandfather read a book to the two young boys, and something remarkable occurred. Three human beings had a great time for two whole hours—together.

It is hard to say who healed the most that day. For, the busy grandfather went back to the hospital the next day. And then the next. And the next. Dozens of books were read. The nurses on the floor started bringing one or two other children into the room in their wheelchairs to listen and heal. When the demand outgrew the capacity of the single hospital room, a larger "reading room" was provided.

Today the grandfather still goes three times a week to the hospital. His flesh-and-blood grandson has long since graduated to the ranks of the healed and healthy, but it makes no difference. There are many other "grandsons" and "granddaughters" who love their Reading Grandfather. The Reading Grandfather still goes to their beds. He touches lives. The life he has touched the most is, of course, his own.

Things, in this world, are not always what they appear to be. Many subtle ironies exist. One such variance is in the principle of giving. It appears to be exporting, but in reality you are importing.

The Reading Grandfather found that out. He is not old. He is not senile. He is not yet even retired. He still runs his company, and he still fights the battles. Over the years he has sat on boards, steered committees, and run a company. He has been praised and named and cited. On the wall of his plush executive office there are numerous plaques that itemize his services. But if you asked him, he would tell you that he'd trade them all for being the hospital's Reading Grandfather. He says, "I used to think I was serving when I sat on the board of a charity or was the chairman of a fund raising effort, but I discovered the fuller dimension. Nothing," he says, "can compare or take the place of one-on-one contact with a child."

He has learned for himself about himself, that he was not meant to be isolated. He has learned that real service means you break through all that and get to people face to face, heart to heart. He has learned service is giving—giving not just time or money— giving self. With his money and his station he had insulated himself from personal service. Giving is personal.

A FINAL WORD

There is one more supreme law of financial freedom. I share it with you in conclusion. In virtually every religious theology extant, there are teachings to the effect that charity is a key to prosperity and an ever-flowing income. I recommend it to you with the added stipulation, (which is not my own, by the way) that you be generous in your almsgiving and that you impart your alms *anonymously*. There is something more than magic that occurs in your life when you do.

People who give money with their name attached do well and accomplish much good. Hundreds of thousands of students have been able to further their educations because of generous grants from individuals and foundations which have been set up in the names of prosperous donors. I wish to take nothing away from such generosity.

Yet, there is something above that level of generosity: quiet, unassuming charity.

There is an art to bestowing your alms on others. There are nearly as many laws and principles in the disposing of money as there are in obtaining it. One of the tricky passages which must be negotiated has to do with creating dependents. You do no person a favor by robbing them of standing on their own legs and walking under their own power. That, too, is an ancient law. Often, loving parents cripple their children in the way they bestow their money on their offspring.

The same thing can happen with people outside your family circle. It is wonderful to assist them in a time of need, but you must be careful not to intervene too early, too often or with too much. The answer is anonymity.

When you bestow gifts of money on others anonymously, you can do it whenever you want, in any amount that you want, to whomever you want. There are no implied obligations and those you help can not become dependent on you. You are free to give and still free after you give. It is better for all concerned.

You will also discover something else. Your joy will be greater. That will be all the reward you could wish for, but it has been my observation that it does not stop there.

The principle, "You cannot give a crust without receiving a loaf in return," will invariably come into effect.

Best of all, you will discover that you can gain more happiness and joy by seeing someone thank someone else, than when they thank you.

Prove the principle for yourself. It may be the single biggest wealth producing thing you ever learn to do. When you give alms anonymously the recipient can only thank the Lord in Heaven; and after all, that is where the thanks truly belongs.

Best wishes, my friend, as you seek financial freedom and may your children be blessed with rich parents!

Appendix A.

Table of Computational Factors

(a) Year	4%	5%	6%	7%	8%	9%	10%	11%	12%	16%	20%
1	1.04	1.05	1.06	1.07	1.08	1.09	1.10	1.11	1.12	1.16	1.20
2	1.08	1.10	1.12	1.14	1.17	1.19	1.21	1.23	1.25	1.35	1.44
3	1.12	1.16	1.19	1.23	1.26	1.30	1.33	1.37	1.40	1.56	1.73
4	1.17	1.22	1.26	1.31	1.36	1.41	1.46	1.52	1.57	1.81	2.07
5	1.22	1.28	1.34	1.40	1.47	1.54	1.61	1.69	1.76	2.10	2.49
6	1.27	1.34	1.42	1.50	1.59	1.68	1.77	1.87	1.97	2.44	2.99
7	1.32	1.41	1.50	1.61	1.71	1.83	1.95	2.08	2.21	2.83	3.58
8	1.37	1.48	1.59	1.72	1.85	1.99	2.14	2.30	2.48	3.28	4.30
9	1.42	1.55	1.69	1.84	2.00	2.17	2.36	2.56	2.77	3.80	5.16
10	1.48	1.63	1.79	1.97	2.16	2.37	2.59	2.84	3.11	4.41	6.19
11	1.54	1.71	1.90	2.10	2.33	2.58	2.85	3.15	3.48	5.12	7.43
12	1.60	1.80	2.01	2.25	2.52	2.81	3.14	3.50	3.90	5.94	8.92
13	1.67	1.89	2.13	2.41	2.72	3.07	3.45	3.88	4.36	6.89	10.70
14	1.73	1.98	2.26	2.58	2.94	3.34	3.80	4.31	4.89	7.99	12.84
15	1.80	2.08	2.40	2.76	3.17	3.64	4.18	4.78	5.47	9.27	15.41
16	1.87	2.18	2.54	2.95	3.43	3.97	4.59	5.31	6.13	10.75	18.49
17	1.95	2.29	2.69	3.16	3.70	4.33	5.05	5.90	6.87	12.47	22.19
18	2.03	2.41	2.85	3.38	4.00	4.72	5.56	6.54	7.69	14.46	26.62
19	2.11	2.53	3.03	3.62	4.32	5.14	6.12	7.26	8.61	16.78	31.95
20	2.19	2.65	3.21	3.87	4.66	5.60	6.73	8.06	9.65	19.46	38.34
23	2.46	3.07	3.82	4.74	5.87	7.26	8.95	11.03	13.55	30.38	66.25
25	2.67	3.39	4.29	5.43	6.85	8.62	10.83	13.59	17.00	40.87	95.40
27	2.88	3.73	4.82	6.21	7.99	10.25	13.11	16.74	21.32	55.00	137.37
30	3.24	4.32	5.74	7.61	10.06	13.27	17.45	22.89	29.96	85.85	237.38
35	3.95	5.52	7.69	10.68	14.79	20.41	28.10	38.57	52.80	180.31	590.67
40	4.80	7.04	10.29	14.97	21.72	31.41	45.26	65.00	93.05	378.72	1469.77
45	5.84	8.99	13.76	21.00	31.92	48.33	72.89	109.53	163.99	795.44	3657.26

FORMULA FOR COMPUTING   **FUTURE VALUE:**   **F = P X CF**

KEY: F = Future Value

P = Present Value (or Principal)

CF = Computational Factor (from Table A above)

APPENDIX B.

How Safe Is Your Bank?

The savings and loan debacle, the largest single financial catastrophe in U.S. history, has sent shock waves through this country and others. In the 1980s dozens of land banks in the midwest and southwest went bankrupt. Forty-five privately-insured financial institutions in the state of Rhode Island were closed. Federal authorities have seized control of once healthy banks, such as the Bank of New England. We live in uncertain and unscrupulous times.

Tragic are the stories of the thousands of innocent men and women who have lost their life's savings in these calamities. Much of the misery could have been averted. Here are some guidelines in determining the stability of financial institutions:

1. LOOK FOR *FEDERAL* DEPOSIT INSURANCE

Since the 1930s, when the Federal Deposit Insurance Corporation (FDIC) was established, no depositor has lost a nickel because of bank default. This agency, backed by the U.S. government, insures that every penny *up to $100,000* will be repaid to the depositor in the event of bank failure.

When your deposits reach the insurance limit, subdivide them and open up accounts in separate banks.

As mentioned earlier in the chapter, I recommend you do that anyway—spread the deposits around. Even when the account is insured, the red-tape and "due process" can tie your funds up for months and can make them inaccessible until all the pontificating and political/legal maneuvering has subsided.

There is an immense difference between federal insurance and *private* insurance. Take note of that. Thousands of people have been burned when, not only their bank went under, but the private insurance carrier behind that institution has gone down in flames along side it.

In summary: (1) Do not place your savings in any institution which is not federally insured. (2) Do not put all your savings in one account, nor in the same institution even if it is federally insured.

As a side note, I once had a woman come up to me in one of my seminars and proudly declare that she agreed with that wisdom and explained how she had gone to the trouble of putting her savings in four *separate branches* of her favorite bank for that very reason. It took me 15 minutes to help her see that I was referring to entirely separate companies not just separate branches of the same bank. (For most of you I hope that anecdote is more amusing than illuminating.)

Sometimes people ask me, "What will happen if the federal government goes under?" "The same thing," I reply, "that would happen if Saturn flew out of its orbit and bashed into the earth, shattering it into micro-fragments; you lose your money." Toning down the sarcasm a notch, I am not saying that I believe the government is infallible or totally invulnerable, but I am saying that within the realm of reasonable possibility, backing by the U.S. government is as safe as you can get.

2. LOOK AT THE BANK OWNERSHIP

The solvency of the bank and the safety of your deposits is largely dependent on the strength of the ownership behind the scenes. Usually it is a holding company. Determine the financial might and stability of the bank's owners before you make your decision. Know who you are really dealing with—the parent company—or the owners. Are they solid? Are they reputable? Are they competent? I am not against the little guy; I root for the underdog unreservedly. But when it comes to your money, you must exercise cold, factual logic. I discourage you from putting your money in small, one- or two-branch banks. They may offer your better interest rates, they may be personable and cordial people, but do they have the strong, diversified financial footing which your life's savings deserve and demand?

In general, a multi-state holding company with a spectrum of diversified assets is preferred. That alone is not the whole answer, but it is a step in the right direction. Even many of the "big boys" are less than invulnerable, but you have more going for you, if they do get in trouble.

3. LOOK AT THE FINANCIAL REPORTS

Go beyond the facades and advertisements. Do a little financial investigation. Banks will provide current financial reports upon request. Get them; and study them. Ask for consolidated financial statements on the holding company and on the bank itself.

Naturally, the first thing you want to know is the *net income* line on the statement. Did the bank turn a profit during the last reporting period? What are the trends? Has it been profitable over the last two or three years? Are the profits increasing, decreasing or staying about the same each quarter? Your bank is a business. If that business is losing money or barely making a profit, that tells you something.

You need to take your analysis a step further. With the information on the financial report and a calculator, you can perform a few simple computations to increase your judgments about the strength of your bank. Here is what to look for:

Capital Ratios

Capital ratios show the shareholders' equity in the company in relation to the assets of the company. There are several to consider.

(1) Equity To Assets

Divide the Shareholders' Equity by the Total Assets:

$$\frac{\text{Shareholders' Equity}}{\text{Total Assets}} = \underline{\hspace{1.5cm}}\%$$

Guideline: Under 4% = Warning. Be careful.

4%-5% = Acceptable

6% and over = Solid

(2) Primary Capital

Slightly more complicated, you simply add Allowance for Loan Losses to the equation in this manner:

$$\frac{\text{Shareholders' Equity + Allowance for Loan Losses}}{\text{Total Assets + Allowance for Loan Losses}} = \underline{\hspace{1.5cm}}\%$$

Guideline: Under 6% = Warning. Be careful.

7% = Acceptable

8% and over = Solid

(3) Loss Allowance To Non-performing Loans

This one may require some digging, but it is worth it. If the information needed to compute this ratio is not provided on the financial statement, request a recent 10K or 10Q report from the bank. Find the amounts for "Non-performing Loans" and "Loans 90-days-or-more Past Due." Then compute as follows:

Allowance For Loan Losses

Non-performing Loans + Loans 90-days-or-more Past Due = __%

Guideline: Under 90% = Warning. Be careful.

90% - 97% = Acceptable

98% and over = Solid

There are no guarantees, but if your bank has good, solid ratios in these areas, it is probably a good choice. There is, however, one other benchmark to consider.

Asset Profile

Statistics can be deceiving. Some banks can exhibit, at present, good ratios but are still in precarious positions. High-risk assets, which are performing, will not send up any red flags on the financial statement until they have tumbled into a past due posture. There is one other important criterion for making a judgment. You will have to request this information from a bank officer; it is not something they usually publish in their brochures.

Ask for the amounts on the following loan or "asset" categories:

1. The Highly-levered Transactions (HLTs)

2. Loans to Less-developed Countries (LDCs)

3. Other Real Estate Owned (OREO)

4. Loans on Commercial Real Estate

These four categories form what I choose to call an "Asset Profile." Add the amounts for these four categories and divide that sum by the Total Shareholders' Equity:

Sum of The Four Categories

Total Shareholders' Equity =_____%

Guideline: 1,000% or over = Warning. Run!

                300% to 1,000% = Risk is moderately high.

                Under 300% = Strong, solid.

Nothing Is Constant

Checking these ratios at the outset—before you deposit your money—is a prudent and wise thing to do. To check these ratios annually—*after* your money is deposited is even wiser. Do not fall asleep. Keep vigil over your precious reservoir. Get the financial reports (often they are mailed to you on a regular basis as a courtesy by the bank) and study them. Compute the ratios and ask the questions. This will take perhaps two hours per year and can save you much anguish and provide you with better sleep at night.

Index

S

T

U

Order Form

Name _____

Company's Name _____

Address _____

City _____ **State** _____ **Zip Code** _____

Daytime Phone _____ **Evening Phone** _____

Please send _____ copies of *Money: An Owner's Manual.*

Please send _____ copies of *"The Money Owner's Kit."*

("The Money Owner's Kit" is a complete set of full size, 8 1/2" x 11" money-management forms **plus** a detailed instruction manual. The kit provides the perfect means to implement the principles taught in *Money: An Owner's Manual.*)

_____ **YES! Add my name to the newsletter mailing list** so that I may receive **free** information about other MMI publications as well as pointers for increased personal productivity.

_____ **YES!** Please send free information about **TimeMax** self-management products.

Item	Quantity	Price	Total
Money: An Owner's Manual		**$11.95**	
"The Money Owners Kit"		**$9.95**	
Subtotal			
Tax (AZ add 6.5%)			
Shipping /Handling (per book)		**$3.50**	
TOTAL			

<u>NOTE</u>: **For orders of more than five books, deduct 5% of the total.**

Telephone orders: Call Toll Free: (800) 622-6463.
    Have your Visa or MasterCard ready.
Fax orders: (602) 545-8233.
 Postal orders: MMI Publishing, 1818 E. Southern Avenue, Mesa, AZ 85204, USA.

Order Form

Name _____

Company's Name _____

Address _____

City _____**State** _____ **Zip Code** _____

Daytime Phone _____**Evening Phone** _____

Please send _____ copies of ***Money: An Owner's Manual.***

Please send _____ copies of ***"The Money Owner's Kit."***

("The Money Owner's Kit" is a complete set of full size, 8 1/2" x 11" money-management forms **plus** a detailed instruction manual. The kit provides the perfect means to implement the principles taught in ***Money: An Owner's Manual.***)

_____**YES! Add my name to the newsletter mailing list** so that I may receive **free** information about other MMI publications as well as pointers for increased personal productivity.

_____**YES!** Please send free information about **TimeMax** self-management products.

Item	Quantity	Price	Total
Money: An Owner's Manual		$11.95	
"The Money Owners Kit"		$9.95	
Subtotal			
Tax (AZ add 6.5%)			
Shipping /Handling (per book)		$3.50	
TOTAL			

<u>NOTE</u>: **For orders of more than five books, deduct 5% of the total.**

Telephone orders: Call Toll Free: (800) 622-6463.
    Have your Visa or MasterCard ready.
Fax orders: (602) 545-8233.
Postal orders: MMI Publishing, 1818 E. Southern Avenue, Mesa, AZ 85204, USA.